No-Guilt Desserts

Most Recipes
200 Calories or Less!

Publications International, Ltd.

Front cover photography by Sanders Studios, Inc.

Pictured on the front cover *(clockwise from top):* Pineapple-Almond Bar *(page 16)*, Cheesecake for One *(page 58)*, Chocolate Chip Cookie *(page 12)*, Black Cherry Freeze *(page 62)* and Orange-Chocolate Bliss *(page 50)*.

Pictured on the back cover *(from top to bottom):* Tri-Layer Chocolate Oatmeal Bars *(page 24)*, Scrumptious Apple Cake *(page 42)*, Fresh Fruit with Peach Glaze *(page 66)* and Marble Cheesecake *(page 56)*.

ISBN: 0-7853-3587-0

Manufactured in U.S.A.

8 7 6 5 4 3 2 1

Nutritional Analysis: The nutritional information that appears with each recipe was submitted in part by the participating companies and associations. Every effort has been made to check the accuracy of these numbers. However, because numerous variables account for a wide range of values for certain foods, nutritive analyses in this book should be considered approximate.

Microwave Cooking: Microwave ovens vary in wattage. Use the cooking times as guidelines and check for doneness before adding more time.

No-Guilt
Desserts

Most Recipes
200 Calories or Less!

Cookies & Brownies

Hershey's 50% Reduced Fat Oatmeal Chip Cookies

¾ cup (1½ sticks) 56-60% vegetable oil spread, softened
¾ cup granulated sugar
¾ cup packed light brown sugar
2 eggs
1 teaspoon vanilla extract
1¼ cups all-purpose flour
1 teaspoon baking soda
½ to ¾ teaspoon ground cinnamon
½ teaspoon salt
2¾ cups quick-cooking rolled oats
2 cups (12-ounce package) HERSHEY'S Reduced Fat Semi-Sweet Baking Chips
1 cup raisins

1. Heat oven to 375°F.

2. In large bowl, beat vegetable oil spread, granulated sugar and brown sugar with electric mixer until well mixed. Add eggs and vanilla; beat until creamy. Stir together flour, baking soda, cinnamon and salt; gradually add to sugar mixture, mixing well. Stir in oats, chips and raisins. Drop by teaspoons onto *ungreased* cookie sheet.

3. Bake 8 to 10 minutes or until golden brown. Cool slightly; remove from cookie sheet to wire rack. Cool completely.
Makes 4 dozen cookies

Nutritional Information per Serving (1 cookie):
Calories: 110, Total Fat: 4 g, Cholesterol: 10 mg, Sodium: 70 mg

Hershey's 50% Reduced Fat Oatmeal Chip Cookies

Mocha Crinkles

1¾ cups all-purpose flour
¾ cup unsweetened cocoa powder
2 teaspoons instant espresso or coffee granules
1 teaspoon baking soda
¼ teaspoon salt
⅛ teaspoon ground black pepper
1⅓ cups packed light brown sugar
½ cup vegetable oil
¼ cup low-fat sour cream
1 egg
1 teaspoon vanilla
½ cup powdered sugar

1. Mix flour, cocoa, espresso, baking soda, salt and pepper in medium bowl; set aside.

2. Beat brown sugar and oil in another medium bowl with electric mixer at medium speed until well blended. Beat in sour cream, egg and vanilla.

3. Beat in flour mixture until soft dough forms. Form dough into disc; cover. Refrigerate dough until firm, 3 to 4 hours.

4. Preheat oven to 350°F. Place powdered sugar in shallow bowl. Cut dough into 1-inch pieces; roll into balls. Coat with powdered sugar. Place on ungreased cookie sheets.

5. Bake 10 to 12 minutes or until tops of cookies are firm to the touch. Do not overbake. Cool cookies completely on wire racks.   *Makes 6 dozen cookies (1 cookie per serving)*

Nutritional Information per Serving: *Calories: 44, Total Fat: 1 g, Cholesterol: 3 mg, Sodium: 28 mg*

Cream Cheese and Jelly Cookies

1 package (8 ounces) reduced-fat cream cheese, softened
¾ cup margarine, softened
2½ teaspoons EQUAL® For Recipes *or* 8 packets EQUAL® sweetener *or* ⅓ cup EQUAL® Spoonful™
2 cups all-purpose flour
¼ teaspoon salt
¼ cup black cherry or seedless raspberry spreadable fruit

• Beat cream cheese, margarine and Equal® in medium bowl until fluffy; mix in flour and salt to form a soft dough. Cover and refrigerate until dough is firm, about 3 hours.

• Roll dough on lightly floured surface into circle ⅛ inch thick; cut into rounds with 3-inch cutter. Place rounded ¼ teaspoon spreadable fruit in center of each round; fold rounds into halves and crimp edges firmly with tines of fork. Pierce tops of cookies with tip of sharp knife. Bake cookies on greased cookie sheets in preheated 350°F oven until lightly browned, about 10 minutes. Cool on wire racks.   *Makes about 3 dozen*

Nutritional Information per Serving (1 cookie): *Calories: 80, Total Fat: 5 g, Cholesterol: 4 mg, Sodium: 78 mg*

Mocha Crinkles

Low Fat Molasses Jumbles

½ cup Prune Purée (recipe follows)
   or prepared prune butter
½ cup sugar
½ cup molasses
1 egg
2 cups all-purpose flour
2 teaspoons ground cinnamon
1 teaspoon ground ginger
½ teaspoon baking soda
½ teaspoon salt
   Additional sugar

Preheat oven to 350°F. Coat baking sheets with vegetable cooking spray. In large bowl, mix prune purée, sugar and molasses until well blended. Add egg; mix well. Combine remaining ingredients except sugar; stir into prune purée mixture just until blended. Roll heaping tablespoonfuls of dough in additional sugar. Place on baking sheets, spacing 2 inches apart. With fork, flatten dough in crisscross fashion until ½ inch thick. Bake in center of oven about 12 to 13 minutes or until set and bottoms are lightly browned. Remove from baking sheets to wire racks to cool completely.

Makes 30 (2½-inch) cookies

Prune Purée

1⅓ cups (8 ounces) pitted prunes
6 tablespoons hot water

Combine pitted prunes and hot water in food processor or blender. Pulse on and off until prunes are finely chopped and smooth. Store leftovers in covered container in refrigerator up to two months.

Makes 1 cup

Nutritional Information per Serving (1 cookie):
Calories: 68, Total Fat: 1 g, Cholesterol: 7 mg, Sodium: 57 mg

Favorite recipe from **California Prune Board**

Soft Apple Cider Cookies

1 cup firmly packed light brown sugar
½ cup FLEISCHMANN'S® 70% Corn Oil
   Spread, softened
½ cup apple cider
½ cup EGG BEATERS® Healthy Real Egg
   Substitute
2¼ cups all-purpose flour
1½ teaspoons ground cinnamon
1 teaspoon baking soda
¼ teaspoon salt
2 medium apples, peeled and diced
   (about 1½ cups)
¾ cup almonds, chopped
   Cider Glaze (recipe follows)

In large bowl, with electric mixer at medium speed, beat sugar and corn oil spread until creamy. Add cider and Egg Beaters®; beat until smooth. With electric mixer at low speed, gradually blend in flour, cinnamon, baking soda and salt. Stir in apples and almonds.

Drop dough by tablespoonfuls, 2 inches apart, onto greased baking sheets. Bake at 375°F for 10 to 12 minutes or until golden brown. Remove from sheets; cool on wire racks. Drizzle with Cider Glaze.

Makes 4 dozen cookies

Prep Time: 30 minutes

Cook Time: 12 minutes

Cider Glaze: In small bowl, combine 1 cup powdered sugar and 2 tablespoons apple cider until smooth.

Nutritional Information per Serving: *Calories: 80, Total Fat: 3 g, Cholesterol: 0 mg, Sodium: 50 mg*

Low Fat Molasses Jumbles

Chocolate Chip Cookies

1½ cups packed light brown sugar
8 tablespoons margarine, softened
2 egg whites
1 teaspoon vanilla
2½ cups all-purpose flour
1½ teaspoons baking soda
½ teaspoon salt
⅓ cup skim milk
¾ cup (4 ounces) semisweet chocolate chips
½ cup chopped pecans or walnuts (optional)

1. Preheat oven to 350°F. Spray cookie sheets with nonstick cooking spray.

2. Beat brown sugar and margarine in large bowl until fluffy. Beat in egg whites and vanilla.

3. Combine flour, baking soda and salt in medium bowl. Add flour mixture to margarine mixture alternately with milk, ending with flour mixture. Stir in chocolate chips and pecans, if desired.

4. Drop dough by slightly rounded tablespoonfuls onto prepared cookie sheets. Bake about 10 minutes or until lightly browned. Cool on wire racks.

Makes about 6 dozen cookies

Nutritional Information per Serving (1 cookie):
Calories: 56, Total Fat: 2 g, Cholesterol: 0 mg, Sodium: 61 mg

Pumpkin Harvest Bars

1¾ cups all-purpose flour
2 teaspoons baking powder
1 teaspoon grated orange peel
1 teaspoon ground cinnamon
½ teaspoon salt
½ teaspoon ground nutmeg
¼ teaspoon ground ginger
¼ teaspoon ground cloves
¾ cup sugar
½ cup MOTT'S® Natural Apple Sauce
½ cup solid-pack pumpkin
1 whole egg
1 egg white
2 tablespoons vegetable oil
½ cup raisins

1. Preheat oven to 350°F. Spray 13×9-inch baking pan with nonstick cooking spray.

2. In small bowl, combine flour, baking powder, orange peel, cinnamon, salt, nutmeg, ginger and cloves.

3. In large bowl, combine sugar, apple sauce, pumpkin, whole egg, egg white and oil.

4. Add flour mixture to apple sauce mixture; stir until well blended. Stir in raisins. Spread batter into prepared pan.

5. Bake 25 to 30 minutes or until toothpick inserted in center comes out clean. Cool on wire rack 15 minutes; cut into 16 bars.

Makes 16 servings

Nutritional Information per Serving: *Calories: 130, Total Fat: 2 g, Cholesterol: 15 mg, Sodium: 110 mg*

Chocolate Chip Cookies

Fabulous Fruit Bars

1½ cups all-purpose flour, divided
1½ cups sugar, divided
½ cup MOTT'S® Apple Sauce, divided
½ teaspoon baking powder
2 tablespoons margarine
½ cup peeled, chopped apple
½ cup chopped dried apricots
½ cup chopped cranberries
1 whole egg
1 egg white
1 teaspoon lemon juice
½ teaspoon vanilla extract
1 teaspoon ground cinnamon

1. Preheat oven to 350°F. Spray 13×9-inch baking pan with nonstick cooking spray.

2. In medium bowl, combine 1¼ cups flour, ½ cup sugar, ⅓ cup apple sauce and baking powder. Cut in margarine with pastry blender or fork until mixture resembles coarse crumbs.

3. In large bowl, combine apple, apricots, cranberries, remaining apple sauce, whole egg, egg white, lemon juice and vanilla.

4. In small bowl, combine remaining 1 cup sugar, ¼ cup flour and cinnamon. Add to fruit mixture, stirring just until mixed.

5. Press half of crumb mixture evenly onto bottom of prepared pan. Top with fruit mixture. Sprinkle with remaining crumb mixture.

6. Bake 40 minutes or until lightly browned. Broil, 4 inches from heat, 1 to 2 minutes or until golden brown. Cool on wire rack 15 minutes; cut into 16 bars.

Makes 16 servings

Nutritional Information per Serving: *Calories: 150, Total Fat: 2 g, Cholesterol: 15 mg, Sodium: 35 mg*

Chewy Coconut Bars

2 eggs
7¼ teaspoons EQUAL® For Recipes *or*
    24 packets EQUAL® sweetener *or*
    1 cup EQUAL® Spoonful™
¼ teaspoon maple flavoring
½ cup margarine, melted
1 teaspoon vanilla
½ cup all-purpose flour
1 teaspoon baking powder
¼ teaspoon salt
1 cup unsweetened coconut,* finely chopped
½ cup chopped walnuts (optional)
½ cup raisins

*Unsweetened coconut can be purchased in health food stores. Or, substitute sweetened coconut and decrease amount of EQUAL® to 5¼ teaspoons EQUAL® For Recipes or 18 packets EQUAL® sweetener or ¾ cup EQUAL® Spoonful™.

• Beat eggs, Equal® and maple flavoring in medium bowl; mix in margarine and vanilla. Combine flour, baking powder and salt in small bowl; stir into egg mixture. Mix in coconut, walnuts and raisins. Spread batter evenly in greased 8-inch square baking pan.

• Bake in preheated 350°F oven until browned and toothpick inserted in center comes out clean, about 20 minutes. Cool in pan on wire rack; cut into squares.

Makes 16 bars

Nutritional Information per Serving (1 bar):
Calories: 126, Total Fat: 9 g, Cholesterol: 27 mg, Sodium: 141 mg

Fabulous Fruit Bars

Lemon Crème Bars

CRUST

2 cups sifted all-purpose flour
¾ cup sifted confectioners' sugar
1 teaspoon grated lemon rind
½ cup unsalted butter, at room temperature
2 tablespoons cold water

LEMON FILLING

½ cup egg substitute *or* 2 large eggs
1¾ cups granulated sugar
¾ cup (3 ounces) shredded ALPINE LACE® Reduced Sodium Muenster Cheese
1½ cups sifted all-purpose flour
1 tablespoon baking powder
⅔ cup fresh lemon juice
1 teaspoon grated lemon rind
¼ cup slivered almonds (optional)
3 tablespoons sifted confectioners' sugar
Additional grated lemon rind (optional)

1. To make the Crust: Preheat the oven to 350°F and butter a 13×9×2-inch baking pan. In a medium-size bowl, mix the flour, confectioners' sugar and lemon rind, then work in the butter with your fingers until coarse crumbs form. Add the water and continue mixing until a dough forms. Press evenly onto the bottom of the baking pan and bake for 10 minutes.

2. While the crust is baking, make the Lemon Filling: In a medium-size bowl, whisk the egg substitute (or the whole eggs) until light yellow. Whisk in the granulated sugar, cheese, flour, baking powder, lemon juice and lemon rind until well blended. Pour the egg mixture over the hot crust and sprinkle with the almonds, if you wish. Return to the oven and bake 25 minutes longer or until the filling is set.

3. Cool the cookies in the pan on a wire rack for 10 minutes, then cut into 36 (2×1½-inch) bars. Cool on wire racks. Dust with the confectioners' sugar. Garnish with additional lemon rind, if you wish. Refrigerate in an airtight container. *Makes 3 dozen bars*

Nutritional Information per Serving (1 bar):
Calories: 105, Total Fat: 3 g, Cholesterol: 9 mg, Sodium: 43 mg

Pineapple-Almond Bars

1 cup all-purpose flour
⅓ cup margarine, melted
¼ cup graham cracker crumbs
¼ cup ground almonds
½ cup sugar, divided
1 package (8 ounces) light cream cheese, softened
1 can (8 ounces) crushed pineapple in juice, drained
¼ cup egg substitute
1 teaspoon almond extract
⅓ cup flaked coconut
¼ cup sliced almonds

1. Preheat oven to 350°F. Combine flour, margarine, graham cracker crumbs, ground almonds and ¼ cup sugar in medium bowl until crumbly. Press onto bottom of 9-inch square pan. Bake 12 minutes.

2. Beat together cream cheese, pineapple, egg substitute, remaining ¼ cup sugar and almond extract in large bowl until blended. Pour over crust. Top with coconut and sliced almonds.

3. Bake 35 to 40 minutes or until golden brown. Cool on wire rack. Refrigerate at least 2 hours. Cut into bars. *Makes 16 bars*

Nutritional Information per serving (1 bar):
Calories: 199, Total Fat: 10 g, Sodium: 111 mg, Cholesterol: 28 mg

Lemon Crème Bars

Brownies

½ cup boiling water
½ cup unsweetened cocoa powder
1¼ cups all-purpose flour
¾ cup granulated sugar
¾ cup packed light brown sugar
1 teaspoon baking powder
¼ teaspoon salt
4 egg whites, lightly beaten
⅓ cup vegetable oil
1½ teaspoons vanilla
½ cup chopped unsalted mixed nuts (optional)

1. Preheat oven to 350°F.

2. Spray 13×9-inch baking pan with nonstick cooking spray. Combine boiling water and cocoa in large bowl. Mix until completely dissolved. Add flour, granulated sugar, brown sugar, baking powder, salt, egg whites, oil and vanilla; mix well. Fold in chopped nuts.

3. Pour mixture into prepared pan. Bake 25 minutes or until brownies spring back when lightly touched. *Do not overbake.* Cool in pan on wire rack; cut into squares.

Makes 32 brownies

Nutritional Information per Serving: *Calories: 81, Total Fat: 2 g, Cholesterol: 0 mg, Sodium: 37 mg*

Granola Bites

2 cups cornflakes cereal
⅔ cup uncooked quick-cooking oats
½ cup chopped pitted dates or raisins
¼ cup 100% bran cereal
½ cup reduced-fat crunchy peanut butter
4 egg whites *or* ½ cup real liquid egg product
5 teaspoons EQUAL® For Recipes *or* 16 packets EQUAL® sweetener *or* ⅔ cup EQUAL® Spoonful™
2 teaspoons vanilla

• Combine cornflakes, oats, dates and bran cereal in large bowl. Mix peanut butter, egg whites, Equal® and vanilla in small bowl until smooth; pour over cereal mixture and stir until all ingredients are coated.

• Shape mixture into 1-inch mounds; place on lightly greased cookie sheets. Bake in preheated 350°F oven until cookies are set and browned, 8 to 10 minutes. Cool on wire racks.

Makes about 2 dozen

Nutritional Information per Serving (1 cookie): *Calories: 67, Total Fat: 3 g, Cholesterol: 0 mg, Sodium: 61 mg*

Brownies

Sunny Cocoa Drop Cookies

½ cup (1 stick) 60% vegetable oil
    spread
⅔ cup granulated sugar
⅔ cup lowfat sour cream
1 egg white
1 teaspoon vanilla extract
¼ teaspoon freshly grated orange peel
1¾ cups all-purpose flour
3 tablespoons HERSHEY'S Cocoa
1 teaspoon baking soda
½ teaspoon baking powder
¼ teaspoon ground cinnamon
    Cocoa Glaze (recipe follows)

1. Heat oven to 350°F. Spray cookie sheet with vegetable cooking spray.

2. Beat vegetable oil spread and granulated sugar in large bowl on medium speed of electric mixer until light and fluffy. Add sour cream, egg white, vanilla and orange peel; beat until well blended. Stir together flour, cocoa, baking soda, baking powder and cinnamon; gradually add to sugar mixture, beating until blended. Drop dough by rounded teaspoons onto prepared cookie sheet.

3. Bake 10 to 12 minutes or until set. Remove from cookie sheet to wire rack. Cool completely. Prepare Cocoa Glaze; drizzle over tops of cookies. Store, covered, at room temperature. *Makes 4 dozen cookies*

Prep Time: 30 minutes
Bake Time: 10 minutes

Nutritional Information per Serving (2 cookies):
Calories: 100, Total Fat: 4 g, Cholesterol: <5 mg, Sodium: 125 mg

Cocoa Glaze

1 tablespoon 60% vegetable oil spread
2 tablespoons water
1 tablespoon HERSHEY'S Cocoa
½ cup powdered sugar
½ teaspoon vanilla extract

Melt vegetable oil spread in small saucepan over low heat. Stir in water and cocoa. Cook, stirring constantly, until thick. *Do not boil.* Remove from heat; gradually add powdered sugar and vanilla, beating with spoon or whisk to drizzling consistency.
Makes about ⅓ cup glaze

Fudgy Peanut Butter Jiffy Cookies

2 cups granulated sugar
½ cup evaporated milk
½ cup (1 stick) margarine or butter
¼ cup unsweetened cocoa powder
2½ cups QUAKER® Oats (quick or old
    fashioned, uncooked)
½ cup peanut butter
½ cup raisins or chopped dates
2 teaspoons vanilla

In large saucepan, combine sugar, milk, margarine and cocoa. Bring to boil over medium heat, stirring frequently. Continue boiling 3 minutes. Remove from heat. Stir in oats, peanut butter, raisins and vanilla; mix well. Quickly drop by tablespoonfuls onto waxed paper or greased cookie sheet. Let stand until set. Store tightly covered at room temperature. *Makes about 3 dozen*

Nutritional Information per Serving (1 cookie):
Calories: 120, Total Fat: 5 g, Cholesterol: 0 mg, Sodium: 55 mg

Sunny Cocoa Drop Cookies

Rocky Road Brownies

BROWNIE

½ cup butter or margarine
3 ounces unsweetened baking chocolate
1 cup all-purpose flour
¾ teaspoon baking powder
½ teaspoon salt
3 eggs
1½ cups DOMINO® Granulated Sugar
1½ teaspoons vanilla

TOPPING

½ cup chopped peanuts
½ cup semi-sweet chocolate chips
½ cup miniature marshmallows
¼ cup chocolate fudge topping, warmed

Heat oven to 350°F. Generously grease 9-inch square baking pan. Melt butter and unsweetened chocolate over low heat in medium saucepan, stirring frequently; cool. Combine flour, baking powder and salt in small bowl; set aside. Beat eggs in large bowl until light. Add sugar, 2 tablespoons at a time, beating until mixture is thick. Add vanilla. Gradually add chocolate mixture to egg mixture. Stir in flour mixture just until blended. Spread evenly into pan. Bake at 350°F for 25 to 30 minutes or until edges slightly pull away from sides of pan. Remove from oven. Sprinkle peanuts, chocolate chips and marshmallows over top; drizzle with chocolate fudge topping. Continue baking 8 to 12 minutes or until lightly browned. Cool completely. Cut into bars.

Makes 2 dozen brownies

Prep Time: 30 minutes
Bake Time: 42 minutes

Nutritional Information per Serving (1 brownie):
Calories: 175, Total Fat: 9 g, Cholesterol: 37 mg, Sodium: 128 mg

Honey Almond Biscotti

½ cup butter or margarine
¾ cup honey
2 eggs
1 teaspoon vanilla
3½ cups all-purpose flour
2 teaspoons ground cinnamon
2 teaspoons aniseeds
½ teaspoon salt
½ teaspoon baking powder
¼ teaspoon baking soda
1 cup dried cranberries or candied cherries
¾ cup slivered almonds

Cream butter in large bowl with electric mixer; beat in honey, eggs and vanilla. Combine flour, cinnamon, aniseeds, salt, baking powder and baking soda in small bowl; mix well. Stir into butter mixture. Stir in cranberries and nuts. Shape dough into two 10×3×1-inch logs on greased baking sheet. Bake in preheated 350°F oven about 20 minutes or until lightly browned. Remove from oven; cool 5 minutes. Remove to cutting board. *Reduce oven temperature to 300°F.* Cut each log into ½-inch strips; place on baking sheet. Bake about 20 minutes more or until crisp throughout. Cool completely on wire racks.

Makes 3 dozen cookies

Nutritional Information per Serving (1 cookie):
Calories: 121, Total Fat: 4 g, Cholesterol: 19 mg, Sodium: 69 mg

Favorite recipe from **National Honey Board**

Marble Brownies

½ cup plus 2 tablespoons all-purpose
  flour, divided
½ cup unsweetened cocoa powder
1 teaspoon baking powder
½ teaspoon salt
1¾ cups sugar, divided
2 tablespoons margarine, softened
½ cup MOTT'S® Natural Apple Sauce
3 egg whites, divided
1½ teaspoons vanilla extract, divided
4 ounces low fat cream cheese
  (Neufchâtel), softened

1. Preheat oven to 350°F. Spray 8-inch square baking pan with nonstick cooking spray.

2. In small bowl, sift together ½ cup flour, cocoa, baking powder and salt.

3. In large bowl, beat 1½ cups sugar and margarine with electric mixer at medium speed until blended. Whisk in apple sauce, 2 egg whites and 1 teaspoon vanilla.

4. Add flour mixture to apple sauce mixture; stir until well blended. Pour batter into prepared pan.

5. In small bowl, beat cream cheese and remaining ¼ cup sugar with electric mixer at medium speed until blended. Stir in remaining egg white, 2 tablespoons flour and ½ teaspoon vanilla. Pour over brownie batter; run knife through batters to marble.

6. Bake 35 to 40 minutes or until firm. Cool on wire rack 15 minutes; cut into 12 bars.
Makes 12 servings

Nutritional Information per Serving: *Calories: 180, Total Fat: 2.5 g, Cholesterol: 0 mg, Sodium: 150 mg*

Frosted Pumpkin Softies

1 cup (2 sticks) margarine or butter,
  softened
¾ cup firmly packed brown sugar
¾ cup granulated sugar
1 cup canned pumpkin
1 egg
1 teaspoon vanilla
2½ cups QUAKER® Oats (quick or old
  fashioned, uncooked)
1¾ cups all-purpose flour
1 teaspoon pumpkin pie spice or
  ground cinnamon
1 teaspoon baking soda
¼ teaspoon salt (optional)

FROSTING

3 ounces cream cheese, softened
1 tablespoon milk
½ teaspoon vanilla
2½ cups powdered sugar
  Yellow and red food coloring
  (optional)

Heat oven to 350°F. Beat together margarine and sugars until creamy. Add pumpkin, egg and vanilla; beat well. Add combined oats, flour, pumpkin pie spice, baking soda and salt; mix well. Drop by rounded tablespoonfuls onto *ungreased* cookie sheet. Bake 11 to 13 minutes or until light golden brown. Cool 1 minute on cookie sheet; remove to wire rack. Cool completely.

For frosting, beat together cream cheese, milk and vanilla until smooth. Gradually beat in powdered sugar until smooth; tint with food color, if desired. Frost top of each cookie. Store in tightly covered container in refrigerator. *Makes about 4 dozen*

Nutritional Information per Serving (1 frosted cookie): *Calories: 130, Total Fat: 5 g, Cholesterol: 5 mg, Sodium: 70 mg*

Tri-Layer Chocolate Oatmeal Bars

CRUST

1 cup uncooked rolled oats
½ cup all-purpose flour
½ cup firmly packed light brown sugar
¼ cup MOTT'S® Natural Apple Sauce
1 tablespoon margarine, melted
¼ teaspoon baking soda

FILLING

⅔ cup all-purpose flour
½ teaspoon baking powder
¼ teaspoon salt
¾ cup granulated sugar
¼ cup MOTT'S® Natural Apple Sauce
1 whole egg
1 egg white
2 tablespoons unsweetened cocoa
    powder
1 tablespoon margarine, melted
½ teaspoon vanilla extract
¼ cup low fat buttermilk

ICING

1 cup powdered sugar
1 tablespoon unsweetened cocoa
    powder
1 tablespoon skim milk
1 teaspoon instant coffee powder

1. Preheat oven to 350°F. Spray 8-inch square baking pan with nonstick cooking spray.

2. To prepare Crust, in medium bowl, combine oats, ½ cup flour, brown sugar, ¼ cup apple sauce, 1 tablespoon margarine and baking soda. Stir with fork until mixture resembles coarse crumbs. Press evenly onto bottom of prepared pan. Bake 10 minutes.

3. To prepare Filling, in small bowl, combine ⅔ cup flour, baking powder and salt.

4. In large bowl, combine granulated sugar, ¼ cup apple sauce, whole egg, egg white, 2 tablespoons cocoa, 1 tablespoon margarine and vanilla.

5. Add flour mixture to apple sauce mixture alternately with buttermilk; stir until well blended. Spread filling over baked crust.

6. Bake 25 minutes or until toothpick inserted in center comes out clean. Cool completely on wire rack.

7. To prepare Icing, in small bowl, combine powdered sugar, 1 tablespoon cocoa, milk and coffee powder until smooth. Spread evenly over bars. Let stand until set. Run tip of knife through icing to score. Cut into 14 bars. *Makes 14 servings*

Nutritional Information per Serving: *Calories: 190, Total Fat: 3 g, Cholesterol: 15 mg, Sodium: 100 mg*

Applesauce Raisin Chews

1 cup (2 sticks) margarine or butter,
    softened
1 cup firmly packed brown sugar
1 cup applesauce
1 egg
1 teaspoon vanilla
2 cups all-purpose flour
1 teaspoon baking soda
1 teaspoon ground cinnamon
½ teaspoon salt (optional)
2½ cups QUAKER® Oats (quick or old
    fashioned, uncooked)
1 cup raisins

Heat oven to 350°F. Beat together margarine and sugar until creamy. Add applesauce, egg and vanilla; beat well. Add combined flour, baking soda, cinnamon and salt; mix well. Stir in oats and raisins. Drop by rounded tablespoonfuls onto *ungreased* cookie sheet. Bake 11 to 13 minutes or until light golden brown. Cool 1 minute on cookie sheet; remove to wire rack. Cool completely. Store in tightly covered container.

Makes about 4 dozen

Nutritional Information per Serving (1 cookie): *Calories: 100, Total Fat: 4 g, Cholesterol: 5 mg, Sodium: 65 mg*

Tri-Layer Chocolate Oatmeal Bars

Chocolate Mousse Squares

¾ cup plus 2 tablespoons all-purpose
   flour, divided
⅔ cup plus 3 tablespoons granulated
   sugar, divided
¼ cup (½ stick) cold margarine
¼ cup HERSHEY'S Cocoa
½ teaspoon powdered instant coffee
¼ teaspoon baking powder
½ cup liquid egg substitute
½ teaspoon vanilla extract
½ cup plain lowfat yogurt
½ teaspoon powdered sugar

Heat oven to 350°F. In medium bowl, stir together ¾ cup flour and 3 tablespoons granulated sugar. With pastry blender or 2 knives, cut in margarine until fine crumbs form. Press mixture onto bottom of *ungreased* 8-inch square baking pan. Bake 15 minutes or until golden. *Reduce oven temperature to 300°F.*

Meanwhile, in small mixer bowl, stir together remaining ⅔ cup granulated sugar, cocoa, remaining 2 tablespoons flour, instant coffee and baking powder. Add egg substitute and vanilla; beat on medium speed of electric mixer until well blended. Add yogurt; beat just until blended. Pour over prepared crust.

Bake 30 minutes or until center is set. Cool completely in pan on wire rack. Cut into squares. If desired, place small paper cutouts over top. Sift powdered sugar over cutouts. Carefully remove cutouts. Store, covered, in refrigerator. *Makes 16 squares*

Nutritional Information per Serving (1 square): *Calories: 100, Total Fat: 3 g, Cholesterol: 0 mg, Sodium: 55 mg*

Oatmeal Raisin Cookies

¼ cup (4 tablespoons) margarine,
   softened
3 tablespoons granulated sugar *or*
   1¼ teaspoons EQUAL® For Recipes
   (5 packets) *or* 2 tablespoons
   fructose
¼ cup egg substitute *or* 2 egg whites
¾ cup unsweetened applesauce
¼ cup frozen unsweetened apple juice
   concentrate, thawed
1 teaspoon vanilla
1 cup all-purpose flour
1 teaspoon baking soda
½ teaspoon ground cinnamon
¼ teaspoon salt (optional)
1½ cups QUAKER® Oats (quick or old
   fashioned, uncooked)
⅓ cup raisins, chopped

Heat oven to 350°F. Lightly spray large cookie sheet with vegetable oil cooking spray. Beat together margarine and sugar until creamy. Beat in egg substitute. Add applesauce, apple juice concentrate and vanilla; beat well. Blend in combined flour, baking soda, cinnamon and salt. Stir in oats and chopped raisins. Drop by rounded teaspoonfuls onto prepared cookie sheet. Bake 15 to 17 minutes or until cookies are firm to the touch and lightly browned. Cool 1 minute on cookie sheet; remove to wire rack. Cool completely. Store in airtight container. *Makes about 3 dozen cookies*

Nutritional Information per Serving (2 cookies made with fructose): *Calories: 110, Total Fat: 3 g, Cholesterol: 0 mg, Sodium: 40 mg*

Chocolate Mousse Squares

Cakes & Pies

Rich Chocolate Cheesecake

1¼ cups graham cracker crumbs
4 tablespoons margarine, melted
1 teaspoon EQUAL® For Recipes *or*
    3 packets EQUAL® sweetener™ *or*
    2 tablespoons EQUAL® Spoonful™
2 packages (8 ounces each) reduced-
    fat cream cheese, softened
1 package (8 ounces) fat-free cream
    cheese, softened
5½ teaspoons EQUAL® For Recipes *or*
    18 packets EQUAL® sweetener *or*
    ¾ cup EQUAL® Spoonful™
2 eggs
2 egg whites
2 tablespoons cornstarch
1 cup reduced-fat sour cream
⅓ cup European or Dutch-process
    cocoa
1 teaspoon vanilla
Fresh mint sprigs, raspberries, nonfat
    whipped topping and orange peel
    (optional)

• Mix graham cracker crumbs, margarine and 1 teaspoon Equal® For Recipes *or* 3 packets Equal® sweetener *or* 2 tablespoons Equal® Spoonful™ in bottom of 9-inch springform pan. Pat mixture evenly on bottom and ½ inch up side of pan.

• Beat cream cheese and 5½ teaspoons Equal® For Recipes *or* 18 packets Equal® sweetener *or* ¾ cup Equal® Spoonful™ in large bowl until fluffy; beat in eggs, egg whites and cornstarch. Mix in sour cream, cocoa and vanilla until well blended. Pour mixture into crust.

• Place cheesecake in roasting pan on oven rack; add 1 inch hot water to roasting pan. Bake cheesecake in preheated 300°F oven just until set in the center, 45 to 50 minutes. Remove cheesecake from roasting pan; return cheesecake to oven. Turn oven off and let cheesecake cool 3 hours in oven with door ajar. Refrigerate 8 hours or overnight. Remove side of pan; place cheesecake on serving plate. Garnish, if desired.

Makes 16 servings

Nutritional Information per Serving: *Calories: 189, Total Fat: 11 g, Cholesterol: 51 mg, Sodium: 280 mg*

Rich Chocolate Cheesecake

Chocolate Cheesecake

24 chocolate wafers, finely crushed
2 to 3 tablespoons water
1 cup nonfat cottage cheese
½ cup EGG BEATERS® Healthy Real Egg Substitute
12 ounces light cream cheese (Neufchâtel), softened
1 cup granulated sugar
½ cup unsweetened cocoa
¼ cup all-purpose flour
1 teaspoon vanilla extract
¾ cup powdered sugar
¾ cup nonfat sour cream
Lavender flowers, for garnish

In small bowl, toss chocolate wafer crumbs with water, 1 tablespoon at a time, until crumbs are moistened. Press onto bottom of 8-inch springform pan; set aside.

In electric blender container or food processor, blend cottage cheese and Egg Beaters® until smooth, scraping down sides of container as necessary. In large bowl, with electric mixer at medium speed, beat cream cheese and granulated sugar until smooth. Add cottage cheese mixture, cocoa, flour and vanilla; beat until well blended and smooth. Pour batter into prepared crust.

Bake at 300°F for 60 to 65 minutes or until puffed and set. Cool in pan on wire rack 15 minutes. Carefully run metal spatula around edge of cheesecake to loosen. Cover; chill at least 4 hours. In small bowl, combine powdered sugar and sour cream. Serve with cheesecake. Garnish with lavender.

Makes 12 servings

Prep Time: 30 minutes

Cook Time: 65 minutes

Nutritional Information per Serving: *Calories: 263, Total Fat: 9 g, Cholesterol: 23 mg, Sodium: 308 mg*

Orange Chiffon Cheesecake

2 cups graham cracker crumbs
8 tablespoons light margarine, melted
1 teaspoon EQUAL® For Recipes or
    3 packets EQUAL® sweetener or
    2 tablespoons EQUAL® Spoonful™
1 cup orange juice
1 envelope (¼ ounce) unflavored gelatin
12 ounces reduced-fat cream cheese, softened
1 cup part-skim ricotta cheese
3½ teaspoons EQUAL® For Recipes or
    12 packets EQUAL® sweetener or
    ½ cup EQUAL® Spoonful™
2 cups light whipped topping
2 medium oranges, peeled, seeded and chopped

• Spray 9-inch springform pan with nonstick cooking spray. Mix graham cracker crumbs, margarine and 1 teaspoon Equal® For Recipes *or* 3 packets Equal® sweetener *or* 2 tablespoons Equal® Spoonful™. Pat mixture evenly on bottom and halfway up side of pan. Bake in preheated 350°F oven 8 to 10 minutes or until set. Cool.

• Pour orange juice into small saucepan. Sprinkle gelatin over orange juice and let soften 1 minute. Heat, stirring constantly, until gelatin dissolves, about 3 minutes. Blend cream cheese and ricotta cheese in large bowl until smooth; stir in 3½ teaspoons Equal® For Recipes *or* 12 packets Equal® sweetener *or* ½ cup Equal® Spoonful™. Add gelatin mixture to cheese mixture; blend until smooth. Fold whipped topping into cheese mixture. Stir in chopped oranges. Spoon into prepared crust and spread evenly.

• Chill 6 hours or overnight. Remove side of pan; place cheesecake on serving plate.

Makes 16 servings

Nutritional Information per Serving: *Calories: 204, Total Fat: 11 g, Cholesterol: 17 mg, Sodium: 209 mg*

New York Cheesecake

1¼ cups vanilla wafer crumbs
4 tablespoons margarine, melted
1 teaspoon EQUAL® For Recipes *or*
    3 packets EQUAL® sweetener *or*
    2 tablespoons EQUAL® Spoonful™
2 packages (8 ounces each) reduced-
    fat cream cheese, softened
1 package (8 ounces) fat-free cream
    cheese, softened
5½ teaspoons EQUAL® For Recipes *or*
    18 packets EQUAL® sweetener *or*
    ¾ cup EQUAL® Spoonful™
2 eggs
2 egg whites
2 tablespoons cornstarch
1 cup reduced-fat sour cream
1 teaspoon vanilla
1 pint strawberries, sliced (optional)
    Strawberry Sauce (recipe follows)

• Mix vanilla wafer crumbs, margarine and 1 teaspoon Equal® For Recipes *or* 3 packets Equal® sweetener *or* 2 tablespoons Equal® Spoonful™ in bottom of 9-inch springform pan. Reserve 1 tablespoon of crumb mixture. Pat remaining mixture evenly on bottom and ½ inch up side of pan. Bake in preheated 350°F oven until crust is lightly browned, about 8 minutes. Cool on wire rack.

• Beat cream cheese and 5½ teaspoons Equal® For Recipes *or* 18 packets Equal® sweetener *or* ¾ cup Equal® Spoonful™ in large bowl until fluffy; beat in eggs, egg whites and cornstarch. Mix in sour cream and vanilla until well blended. Pour mixture into crust.

• Place cheesecake in roasting pan on oven rack; add 1 inch hot water to roasting pan. Bake in preheated 300°F oven just until set in the center, 45 to 60 minutes. Remove cheesecake from roasting pan, sprinkle with reserved crumb mixture and return to oven. Turn oven off and let cheesecake cool 3 hours in oven with door ajar. Refrigerate 8 hours or overnight.

• Remove side of pan; place cheesecake on serving plate. Serve with strawberries and Strawberry Sauce.   *Makes 16 servings*

Nutritional Information per Serving: *Calories: 187, Total Fat: 12 g, Cholesterol: 56 mg, Sodium: 253 mg*

Strawberry Sauce

1 package (16 ounces) frozen
    unsweetened strawberries, thawed
1 tablespoon lemon juice
1¾ teaspoons EQUAL® For Recipes *or*
    6 packets EQUAL® sweetener *or*
    ¼ cup EQUAL® Spoonful™

• Process strawberries in food processor or blender until smooth. Stir in lemon juice and Equal®; refrigerate until serving time.
          Makes about 2 cups

Nutritional Information per Serving (2 tablespoons): *Calories: 12, Total Fat: 0 g, Cholesterol: 0 mg, Sodium: 1 mg*

Turtle Cheesecake

6 tablespoons reduced-calorie
   margarine
1½ cups graham cracker crumbs
2 envelopes unflavored gelatin
2 packages (8 ounces each) fat-free
   cream cheese
2 cups 1% low-fat cottage cheese
1 cup sugar
1½ teaspoons vanilla
1 container (8 ounces) thawed
   reduced-fat nondairy whipped
   topping
¼ cup prepared fat-free caramel
   topping
¼ cup prepared fat-free hot fudge
   topping
¼ cup chopped pecans

1. Preheat oven to 350°F. Spray bottom and side of 9-inch springform pan with nonstick cooking spray. Melt margarine in small saucepan over medium heat. Stir in graham cracker crumbs. Press crumb mixture firmly onto bottom and side of prepared pan. Bake 10 minutes. Cool.

2. Place ½ cup cold water in small saucepan; sprinkle gelatin over water. Let stand 3 minutes to soften. Heat gelatin mixture over low heat until completely dissolved, stirring constantly.

3. Combine cream cheese, cottage cheese, sugar and vanilla in food processor or blender; process until smooth. Add gelatin mixture; process until well blended. Fold in whipped topping. Pour into prepared crust. Refrigerate 4 hours or until set.

4. Loosen cake from side of pan. Remove side of pan from cake. Drizzle caramel and hot fudge toppings over cake. Sprinkle pecans evenly over top of cake before serving. *Makes 16 servings*

Nutritional Information per Serving: *Calories: 231, Total Fat: 7 g, Cholesterol: 1 mg, Sodium: 419 mg*

Luscious Chocolate Cheesecake

2 cups (16 ounces) nonfat cottage
   cheese
¾ cup frozen egg substitute, thawed
⅔ cup sugar
4 ounces (½ of 8-ounce package)
   Neufchâtel cheese (light cream
   cheese), softened
⅓ cup HERSHEY'S Cocoa or HERSHEY'S
   European Style Cocoa
½ teaspoon vanilla extract
   Yogurt Topping (recipe follows)
   Sliced strawberries or mandarin
   orange segments (optional)

Heat oven to 300°F. Spray 9-inch springform pan with vegetable cooking spray. In food processor, place cottage cheese, egg substitute, sugar, Neufchâtel cheese, cocoa and vanilla; process until smooth. Pour into prepared pan.

Bake 35 minutes or until edge is set. Meanwhile, prepare Yogurt Topping. Carefully spread topping over top of warm cheesecake. Return cheesecake to oven; bake 5 minutes. With knife, loosen cheesecake from side of pan. Cool completely in pan on wire rack. Cover; refrigerate until chilled. Just before serving, remove side of pan. Serve with strawberries or oranges, if desired. Garnish as desired. Cover; refrigerate leftover cheesecake. *Makes 9 servings*

Yogurt Topping: In small bowl, stir together ⅔ cup plain nonfat yogurt and 2 tablespoons sugar until well blended.

Nutritional Information per Serving: *Calories: 170, Total Fat: 5 g, Cholesterol: 10 mg, Sodium: 290 mg*

Turtle Cheesecake

Mocha Marble Pound Cake

2 cups all-purpose flour
2 teaspoons baking powder
1 teaspoon baking soda
½ teaspoon salt
1 cup sugar
¼ cup FLEISCHMANN'S® 70% Corn Oil
    Spread, softened
1 teaspoon vanilla extract
½ cup EGG BEATERS® Healthy Real Egg
    Substitute
1 (8-ounce) container low fat coffee
    yogurt
¼ cup unsweetened cocoa
    Mocha Yogurt Glaze (recipe follows)

In small bowl, combine flour, baking powder, baking soda and salt; set aside.

In large bowl, with electric mixer at medium speed, beat sugar, corn oil spread and vanilla until creamy. Add Egg Beaters®; beat until smooth. With mixer at low speed, add yogurt alternately with flour mixture, beating well after each addition. Remove half of batter to medium bowl. Add cocoa to batter remaining in large bowl; beat until blended. Alternately spoon coffee and chocolate batters into greased 9×5×3-inch loaf pan. With knife, cut through batters to create marbled effect.

Bake at 325°F for 60 to 65 minutes or until toothpick inserted in center comes out clean. Cool in pan on wire rack for 10 minutes. Remove from pan; cool completely on wire rack. Frost with Mocha Yogurt Glaze.   *Makes 16 servings*

Mocha Yogurt Glaze: In small bowl, combine ½ cup powdered sugar, 1 tablespoon unsweetened cocoa and 1 tablespoon low fat coffee yogurt until smooth; add more yogurt if necessary to make spreading consistency.

Nutritional Information per Serving: *Calories: 159, Total Fat: 3 g, Cholesterol: 1 mg, Sodium: 215 mg*

Marbled Angel Cake

1 package (about 15 ounces) angel
    food cake mix
¼ cup HERSHEY₀S Cocoa
    Chocolate Glaze (recipe follows)

Place oven rack in lowest position. Heat oven to 375°F. Prepare cake batter as directed on package. Transfer 4 cups batter to medium bowl; gradually fold in cocoa until well blended, being careful not to deflate batter. Alternately pour vanilla and chocolate batters into ungreased 10-inch tube pan. With knife or metal spatula, cut through batters for marble effect.

Bake 30 to 35 minutes or until top crust is firm and looks very dry. *Do not underbake.* Invert pan on heatproof funnel or bottle; cool completely, at least 1½ hours. Carefully run knife along side of pan to loosen cake; remove from pan. Place on serving plate; drizzle with Chocolate Glaze. Let stand until set. Store, covered, at room temperature.
                    Makes 16 servings

Chocolate Glaze: In small saucepan, combine ⅓ cup sugar and ¼ cup water. Cook over medium heat, stirring constantly, until mixture comes to a boil. Stir until sugar dissolves; remove from heat. Immediately add 1 cup HERSHEY₀S MINI CHIPS Semi-Sweet Chocolate; stir until chips are melted and mixture is smooth. Cool to desired consistency; use immediately.

Nutritional Information per Serving: *Calories: 180, Total Fat: 4 g, Cholesterol: 0 mg, Sodium: 200 mg*

Banana Orange Muffincake

MUFFINCAKE
1½ cups all-purpose flour
1 cup QUAKER® Oats (quick or old fashioned, uncooked)
⅓ cup firmly packed brown sugar
1 tablespoon baking powder
½ teaspoon baking soda
¼ teaspoon salt (optional)
⅔ cup mashed banana (about 2 small)
½ cup orange juice
⅓ cup (5⅓ tablespoons) margarine, melted
2 egg whites *or* 1 egg, slightly beaten
½ teaspoon grated orange peel

GLAZE
½ cup powdered sugar
1 tablespoon orange juice
½ teaspoon grated orange peel

Heat oven to 400°F. Spray bottom of 9-inch springform or round cake pan with no-stick cooking spray or grease lightly. For muffincake, combine dry ingredients; mix well. Add combined banana, orange juice, margarine, egg whites and orange peel, mixing just until moistened. Pour into prepared pan. Bake 30 to 35 minutes or until golden brown. Cool 10 minutes on wire rack; remove from pan. For glaze, combine all ingredients; mix until smooth. Drizzle evenly over warm muffincake.

Makes 12 servings

Variation: To make muffins, line 12 medium muffin cups with paper baking cups or spray with no-stick cooking spray. Prepare batter as directed. Fill muffin cups almost full. Bake 15 to 18 minutes or until golden brown. Prepare glaze as directed above; drizzle over warm muffins.

Nutritional Information per Serving: *Calories: 160, Total Fat: 2 g, Cholesterol: 10 mg, Sodium: 140 mg*

Apple-Streusel Pound Cake

3 cups all-purpose flour
⅓ cup cornmeal
1½ teaspoons baking soda
1½ teaspoons baking powder
½ teaspoon salt
1 cup granulated sugar
1 cup skim milk
1 cup nonfat sour cream
½ cup MOTT'S® Natural Apple Sauce
1 whole egg
2 tablespoons vegetable oil
2 teaspoons vanilla extract
3 egg whites, beaten until stiff
¾ cup firmly packed light brown sugar
¾ cup chopped peeled apple
½ cup uncooked rolled oats
2 teaspoons ground cinnamon

1. Preheat oven to 350°F. Spray 10-inch (12-cup) Bundt pan with nonstick cooking spray; flour lightly.

2. In medium bowl, combine 3 cups flour, cornmeal, baking soda, baking powder and salt.

3. In large bowl, combine granulated sugar, milk, sour cream, apple sauce, whole egg, oil and vanilla.

4. Add flour mixture to apple sauce mixture; stir until well blended. Gently fold in beaten egg whites.

5. In small bowl, combine brown sugar, apple, oats and cinnamon.

6. Spread half of batter into prepared pan; sprinkle with oat mixture. Spread remaining batter over oat mixture.

7. Bake 60 to 70 minutes or until toothpick inserted in center comes out clean. Cool on wire rack 15 minutes before removing from pan. Place cake, fluted side up, on serving plate. Serve warm or cool completely. Cut into 24 slices. *Makes 24 servings*

Nutritional Information per Serving: *Calories: 170, Total Fat: 2 g, Cholesterol: 10 mg, Sodium: 110 mg*

Brownie Cake Delight

1 package reduced-fat fudge brownie mix
⅓ cup strawberry all-fruit spread
2 cups thawed reduced-fat nondairy whipped topping
¼ teaspoon almond extract
2 cups strawberries, stems removed and cut into halves
¼ cup chocolate sauce

1. Prepare brownies according to package directions, substituting 11×7-inch baking pan. Cool completely in pan.

2. Whisk fruit spread in small bowl until smooth.

3. Combine whipped topping and almond extract in medium bowl.

4. Cut brownie crosswise in half. Place half of brownie, flat-side down, on serving dish. Spread with fruit spread and 1 cup whipped topping. Place second half of brownie, flat-side down, over bottom layer. Spread with remaining whipped topping. Arrange strawberries on whipped topping. Drizzle chocolate sauce onto cake before serving. Garnish with fresh mint, if desired.

Makes 16 servings

Nutritional Information per Serving: *Calories: 193, Total Fat: 3 g, Cholesterol: trace, Sodium: 140 mg*

Light & Luscious Chocolate Cake with Raspberry Sauce

2 cups all-purpose flour
1⅓ cups skim milk
1 cup sugar
1 cup EGG BEATERS® Healthy Real Egg Substitute
⅔ cup unsweetened cocoa
⅔ cup FLEISCHMANN'S® 70% Corn Oil Spread, softened
1½ teaspoons baking powder
1½ teaspoons vanilla extract
½ teaspoon baking soda
Raspberry Sauce (recipe follows)
Fresh raspberries and fresh mint sprigs, for garnish

In large bowl, with electric mixer at medium speed, combine flour, milk, sugar, Egg Beaters®, cocoa, corn oil spread, baking powder, vanilla and baking soda just until blended. Beat at high speed for 3 minutes. Spread batter into lightly greased 13×9×2-inch baking pan. Bake at 350°F for 30 to 35 minutes or until toothpick inserted in center comes out clean. Cool in pan on wire rack. Cut into 16 (3×2-inch) pieces. Serve topped with Raspberry Sauce. Garnish with raspberries and mint. *Makes 16 servings*

Prep Time: 20 minutes

Cook Time: 35 minutes

Raspberry Sauce: In electric blender container, purée 2 cups thawed frozen raspberries in syrup; strain. Stir in 2 tablespoons sugar and 1 tablespoon cornstarch. In small saucepan, cook raspberry mixture until thickened and boiling. Cover; chill.

Nutritional Information per Serving (1 piece cake, 2 tablespoons sauce): *Calories: 238, Total Fat: 8 g, Cholesterol: 0 mg, Sodium: 161 mg*

Brownie Cake Delight

Pineapple Upside-Down Cake

1 can (14 ounces) unsweetened crushed pineapple in juice, undrained
¼ cup pecan pieces (optional)
2 tablespoons lemon juice, divided
1¾ teaspoons EQUAL® For Recipes *or* **6 packets EQUAL® sweetener** *or* **¼ cup EQUAL® Spoonful™**
1 teaspoon cornstarch
4 tablespoons margarine, at room temperature
3½ teaspoons EQUAL® For Recipes *or* **12 packets EQUAL® sweetener** *or* **½ cup EQUAL® Spoonful™**
1 egg
1 cup cake flour
1½ teaspoons baking powder
½ teaspoon baking soda
¼ teaspoon ground cinnamon
¼ teaspoon ground nutmeg
⅛ teaspoon ground ginger
⅓ cup buttermilk

• Drain pineapple, reserving ¼ cup juice. Mix pineapple, pecans, 1 tablespoon lemon juice, 1¾ teaspoons Equal® For Recipes *or* 6 packets Equal® sweetener *or* ¼ cup Equal® Spoonful™ and cornstarch in bottom of 8-inch square or 9-inch round cake pan; spread mixture evenly in pan.

• Beat margarine and 3½ teaspoons Equal® For Recipes *or* 12 packets Equal® sweetener *or* ½ cup Equal® Spoonful™ in medium bowl until fluffy; beat in egg. Combine flour, baking powder, baking soda and spices in small bowl. Add to margarine mixture alternately with buttermilk, ¼ cup reserved pineapple juice and remaining 1 tablespoon lemon juice, beginning and ending with dry ingredients. Spread batter over pineapple mixture in cake pan.

• Bake in preheated 350°F oven until browned and toothpick inserted in center comes out clean, about 25 minutes.

• Invert cake immediately onto serving plate. Serve warm or at room temperature.
Makes 8 servings

Note: If desired, maraschino cherry halves may be placed on bottom of cake pan with pineapple mixture.

Nutritional Information per Serving: *Calories: 156, Total Fat: 7 g, Cholesterol: 27 mg, Sodium: 257 mg*

Blueberry Angel Food Cake Rolls

1 package DUNCAN HINES® Angel Food Cake Mix
Confectioners' sugar
1 can (21 ounces) blueberry pie filling
¼ cup confectioners' sugar
Mint leaves, for garnish (optional)

1. Preheat oven to 350°F. Line two 15½×10½×1-inch jelly-roll pans with aluminum foil.

2. Prepare cake following package directions. Divide into pans. Spread evenly. Cut through batter with knife or spatula to remove large air bubbles. Bake at 350°F for 15 minutes or until set. Invert cakes at once onto clean, lint-free dish towels dusted with confectioners' sugar. Remove foil carefully. Roll up each cake with towel jelly-roll fashion, starting at short end. Cool completely.

3. Unroll cakes. Spread about 1 cup blueberry pie filling to within 1 inch of edges on each cake. Reroll and place seam side down on serving plate. Dust with ¼ cup confectioners' sugar. Garnish with mint leaves, if desired.
Makes 2 cakes (8 servings each)

Nutritional Information per Serving: *Calories: 143, Total Fat: 0 g, Cholesterol: 0 mg, Sodium: 77 mg*

Pineapple Upside-Down Cake

Easy Carrot Cake

½ cup Prune Purée (recipe follows)
2 cups all-purpose flour
2 teaspoons ground cinnamon
1½ teaspoons baking soda
½ teaspoon salt
4 cups shredded DOLE® Carrots
2 cups sugar
½ cup DOLE® Pineapple Juice
2 eggs
2 teaspoons vanilla extract
Vegetable cooking spray

• **Prepare** Prune Purée; set aside.

• **Combine** flour, cinnamon, baking soda and salt in medium bowl; set aside.

• **Beat** together Prune Purée, carrots, sugar, juice, eggs and vanilla in large bowl until blended. Add flour mixture; stir until well blended.

• **Spread** batter into 13×9-inch baking dish sprayed with vegetable cooking spray.

• **Bake** at 375°F 30 to 35 minutes or until toothpick inserted in center comes out clean. Cool completely in dish on wire rack. Dust with powdered sugar and garnish with carrot curls, if desired. *Makes 12 servings*

Prep Time: 15 minutes

Bake Time: 35 minutes

Prune Purée: Combine 1⅓ cups DOLE® Pitted Prunes, halved, and ½ cup hot water in food processor or blender container. Process until prunes are finely chopped, stopping to scrape down side occasionally. (Purée can be refrigerated in airtight container for up to 1 week.)

Nutritional Information per Serving: *Calories: 240, Total Fat: 1 g, Cholesterol: 32 mg, Sodium: 244 mg*

Spice Cake with Fresh Peach Sauce

CAKE:

1 package DUNCAN HINES® Moist Deluxe Spice Cake Mix
3 egg whites
1¼ cups water
⅓ cup vegetable oil

SAUCE:

6 cups sliced fresh peaches
1 cup water
⅓ cup sugar
⅛ teaspoon ground cinnamon

1. Preheat oven to 350°F. Grease and flour 10-inch bundt or tube pan.

2. For Cake, place cake mix, egg whites, water and oil in large bowl. Beat at low speed with electric mixer until blended. Beat at medium speed 2 minutes. Bake at 350°F for 42 to 47 minutes or until toothpick inserted in center comes out clean. Cool in pan 25 minutes. Invert onto serving plate. Cool completely. Dust with confectioners' sugar, if desired.

2. For Sauce, combine peaches and water in large saucepan. Cook over medium heat 5 minutes. Reduce heat to low. Cover and simmer 10 minutes. Cool. Reserve ½ cup peach slices. Combine remaining peaches with any cooking liquid, sugar and cinnamon in blender or food processor. Process until smooth. Stir in reserved peach slices. To serve, spoon peach sauce over cake slices. *Makes 12 to 16 servings*

Tip: Fresh peach sauce can be served either warm or chilled.

Note: Use ¾ cup egg substitute in place of egg whites, if desired.

Nutritional Information per Serving: *Calories: 299, Total Fat: 10 g, Cholesterol: 0 mg, Sodium: 294 mg*

Blueberry Lattice Pie

6 cups fresh blueberries *or* **2 packages (16 ounces each) frozen unsweetened blueberries**
3 tablespoons lemon juice
6 tablespoons cornstarch
8 teaspoons EQUAL® For Recipes *or* **27 packets EQUAL® sweetener** *or* **1 cup plus 2 tablespoons EQUAL® Spoonful™**
Reduced-Fat Pie Pastry (recipe follows), 2 recipes for double crust or favorite pastry for double crust 9-inch pie

• Toss blueberries and lemon juice in large bowl. Sprinkle with combined cornstarch and Equal® and toss to coat. Let stand 30 minutes.

• Roll half of pastry on lightly floured surface into circle 1 inch larger than inverted 9-inch pie pan. Ease pastry into pan; trim within 1 inch of edge of pan. Roll remaining pastry to ⅛-inch thickness; cut into 10 to 12 strips, ½ inch wide.

• Pour blueberry mixture into pastry. Arrange pastry strips over filling and weave into lattice design. Trim ends of lattice strips; fold edge of lower crust over ends of lattice strips. Seal and flute edge.

• Bake in preheated 425°F oven until crust is browned and filling is bubbly, about 1 hour. Cover edge of crust with aluminum foil if browning too quickly. Cool on wire rack; refrigerate leftovers.   *Makes 8 servings*

Nutritional Information per Serving: *Calories: 345, Total Fat: 12 g, Cholesterol: 0 mg, Sodium: 143 mg*

Reduced-Fat Pie Pastry

1¼ cups all-purpose flour
1 teaspoon EQUAL® For Recipes *or* **3 packets EQUAL® sweetener** *or* **2 tablespoons EQUAL® Spoonful™**
¼ teaspoon salt
4 tablespoons cold margarine, cut into pieces
5 to 5½ tablespoons ice water

• Combine flour, Equal® and salt in medium bowl; cut in margarine with pastry blender until mixture resembles coarse crumbs. Mix in water, 1 tablespoon at a time, stirring lightly with fork after each addition until dough is formed. Wrap and refrigerate until ready to use.

• For prebaked crust, roll pastry on lightly floured surface into circle 1 inch larger than inverted 9-inch pie pan. Ease pastry into pan; trim and flute edge. Pierce bottom and side of pastry with fork. Bake in preheated 425°F oven until pastry is browned, 10 to 15 minutes. Cool on wire rack.
Makes pastry for 9-inch pie (8 servings)

Tip: Double recipe for double crust or lattice pies.

Nutritional Information per Serving: *Calories: 123, Total Fat: 6 g, Cholesterol: 0 mg, Sodium: 134 mg*

Scrumptious Apple Cake

3 egg whites
1½ cups sugar
1 cup unsweetened applesauce
1 teaspoon vanilla
2 cups all-purpose flour
2 teaspoons ground cinnamon
1 teaspoon baking soda
¼ teaspoon salt
4 cups cored peeled tart apple slices
    (McIntosh or Crispin)
Yogurt Glaze (recipe follows)

Preheat oven to 350°F. Beat egg whites until slightly foamy; add sugar, applesauce and vanilla. Combine flour, cinnamon, baking soda and salt in separate bowl; add to applesauce mixture. Spread apples in 13×9-inch pan or 9-inch round springform pan sprayed with nonstick cooking spray. Spread batter over apples. Bake 35 to 40 minutes or until toothpick inserted in center comes out clean; cool on wire rack. Prepare Yogurt Glaze; spread over cooled cake.
Makes 15 to 20 servings

Yogurt Glaze: Combine 1½ cups plain or vanilla nonfat yogurt, 3 tablespoons brown sugar (or to taste) and 1 teaspoon vanilla or 1 teaspoon lemon juice. Stir together until smooth.

Nutritional Information per Serving: *Calories: 170, Total Fat: trace, Cholesterol: 1 mg, Sodium: 130 mg*

Favorite recipe from **New York Apple Association, Inc.**

Four Way Fudgey Chocolate Cake

1¼ cups all-purpose flour
1 cup sugar
1 cup skim milk
⅓ cup HERSHEY'S Cocoa or HERSHEY'S Dutch Processed Cocoa
⅓ cup unsweetened applesauce
1 tablespoon white vinegar
1 teaspoon baking soda
½ teaspoon vanilla extract
Toppings (optional): Frozen light non-dairy whipped topping, thawed, REESE'S® Peanut Butter Chips, sliced strawberries, chopped almonds, raspberries

Heat oven to 350°F. Spray 9-inch square baking pan or 11×7×2-inch baking pan with vegetable cooking spray. In large mixer bowl, stir together flour, sugar, milk, cocoa, applesauce, vinegar, baking soda and vanilla; beat on low speed of electric mixer until blended. Pour batter into prepared pan. Bake 30 to 35 minutes or until wooden pick inserted in center comes out clean. Cool completely in pan on wire rack. Spoon whipped topping into pastry bag fitted with star tip; pipe stars in two lines to divide cake into four squares or rectangles. Using plain tip, pipe lattice design into one square; place peanut butter chips onto lattice. Place strawberries into another square. Sprinkle almonds into third square. Place raspberries into remaining square. Serve immediately. Cover; refrigerate leftover cake. Store ungarnished cake, covered, at room temperature.
Makes 12 servings

Nutritional Information per Serving (no garnishes): *Calories: 130, Total Fat: 0 g, Cholesterol: 0 mg, Sodium: 80 mg*

Scrumptious Apple Cake

Mile-High Apple Pie

Reduced-Fat Pie Pastry (2 recipes for double crust, page 41) or favorite pastry for double crust 9-inch pie
3 tablespoons cornstarch
7¼ teaspoons EQUAL® For Recipes or
    24 packets EQUAL® sweetener or
    1 cup EQUAL® Spoonful™
¾ teaspoon ground cinnamon
¼ teaspoon salt
¼ teaspoon ground nutmeg
8 cups sliced cored peeled Granny Smith or other baking apples (about 8 medium)

• Roll half the pastry on floured surface into circle 1 inch larger than inverted 9-inch pie pan. Ease pastry into pan.

• Combine cornstarch, Equal®, cinnamon, salt and nutmeg; sprinkle over apples in large bowl and toss. Arrange apple mixture in pie crust.

• Roll remaining pastry into circle large enough to fit top of pie. Cut out hearts from pastry with cookie cutters. Place remaining pastry on pie; seal edges, trim and flute. Press heart cut-outs on pastry. Bake in preheated 425°F oven until pastry is golden and apples are tender, 40 to 50 minutes. Cool on wire rack.   *Makes 8 servings*

Nutritional Information per Serving: *Calories: 334, Total Fat: 12 g, Cholesterol: 0 mg, Sodium: 335 mg*

Key Lime Pie

1 cup graham cracker crumbs
3 tablespoons melted margarine
1 teaspoon EQUAL® For Recipes or
    3 packets EQUAL® sweetener or
    2 tablespoons EQUAL® Spoonful™
1 envelope (¼ ounce) unflavored gelatin
1¾ cups skim milk, divided
1 package (8 ounces) reduced-fat cream cheese, softened
⅓ to ½ cup fresh lime juice
3½ teaspoons EQUAL® For Recipes or
    12 packets EQUAL® sweetener or
    ½ cup EQUAL® Spoonful™
Lime slices, raspberries and fresh mint sprigs, for garnish (optional)

• Combine graham cracker crumbs, margarine and 1 teaspoon Equal® For Recipes or 3 packets Equal® sweetener or 2 tablespoons Equal® Spoonful™ in bottom of 7-inch springform pan; pat evenly on bottom and ½ inch up side of pan.

• Sprinkle gelatin over ½ cup milk in small saucepan; let stand 2 to 3 minutes. Cook over low heat, stirring constantly, until gelatin is dissolved. Beat cream cheese in small bowl until fluffy; beat in remaining 1¼ cups milk and gelatin mixture. Mix in lime juice and 3½ teaspoons Equal® For Recipes or 12 packets Equal® sweetener or ½ cup Equal® Spoonful™. Refrigerate pie until set, about 2 hours.

• To serve, loosen side of pie from pan with small spatula and remove side of pan. Place pie on serving plate; garnish with lime slices, raspberries and mint, if desired.
        Makes 8 servings

Nutritional Information per Serving: *Calories: 150, Total Fat: 10 g, Cholesterol: 16 mg, Sodium: 231 mg*

Mile-High Apple Pie

Chocolate Roulade with Creamy Yogurt Filling

Creamy Yogurt Filling (recipe follows)
3 egg whites
½ cup granulated sugar, divided
1 container (8 ounces) liquid egg substitute
½ cup cake flour
¼ cup HERSHEY₅S Cocoa
1 teaspoon baking powder
⅛ teaspoon salt
2 tablespoons water
1 teaspoon vanilla extract
2 teaspoons powdered sugar
Peach Sauce (recipe follows)

Prepare Creamy Yogurt Filling. Heat oven to 375°F. Line 15½×10½×1-inch jelly-roll pan with foil; spray with vegetable cooking spray. In large mixer bowl, beat egg whites on high speed of electric mixer until foamy; gradually add ¼ cup granulated sugar, beating well after each addition until stiff peaks hold their shape, sugar is dissolved and mixture is glossy. In small mixer bowl, beat egg substitute on medium speed until foamy; gradually add remaining ¼ cup granulated sugar, beating until mixture is thick. Fold egg substitute mixture into egg white mixture. In another small bowl, stir together flour, cocoa, baking powder and salt; gently fold into egg mixture alternately with water and vanilla. Spread batter evenly into prepared pan.

Bake 10 to 12 minutes or until top springs back when touched lightly in center. Immediately invert onto clean, lint-free dishtowel sprinkled with powdered sugar; peel off foil. Starting at narrow end, roll up cake and towel together. Cool completely on wire rack. Unroll cake; remove towel. Spread with Creamy Yogurt Filling to within ½ inch of edges of cake. Reroll cake; place, seam-side down, on serving plate. Cover;

refrigerate 2 to 3 hours or until chilled before serving. (Cake should be eaten same day as prepared.) Serve with Peach Sauce. Garnish as desired. *Makes 10 servings*

Nutritional Information per Serving: *Calories: 140, Total Fat: 1 g, Cholesterol: 0 mg, Sodium: 130 mg*

Creamy Yogurt Filling

Yogurt Cheese (recipe follows)
1 envelope (1.3 ounces) dry whipped topping mix
⅓ cup cold skim milk
1 teaspoon vanilla extract
⅛ to ¼ teaspoon almond extract

Prepare Yogurt Cheese (recipe follows). Prepare topping mix as directed on package, using ⅓ cup milk, 1 teaspoon vanilla and almond extract. Gently fold Yogurt Cheese into whipped topping.

Yogurt Cheese: Use one 8-ounce container plain nonfat yogurt, no gelatin added. Line non-rusting colander or sieve with large piece of double thickness cheesecloth or large coffee filter; place colander over deep bowl. Spoon yogurt into prepared colander; cover with plastic wrap. Refrigerate until liquid no longer drains from yogurt, about 24 hours. Remove yogurt from cheesecloth and place in separate bowl; discard liquid.

Peach Sauce: In blender container, place 1½ cups fresh peach slices and 1 tablespoon sugar. Cover; blend until smooth. In medium microwave-safe bowl, stir together ¼ cup water and 1½ teaspoons cornstarch until dissolved. Add peach mixture; stir. Microwave at HIGH (100%) 2½ to 3 minutes or until mixture boils and thickens, stirring after each minute. Cool completely.

Magic Apple Roll

2 cups MOTT'S® Natural Apple Sauce
½ teaspoon ground cinnamon
4 egg whites
¾ cup granulated sugar
⅔ cup all-purpose flour
¾ teaspoon baking powder
¼ teaspoon salt
1 teaspoon vanilla extract
1 tablespoon powdered sugar

1. Preheat oven to 400°F. Spray 15×10-inch jelly-roll pan with nonstick cooking spray. Line with waxed paper; spray paper with cooking spray. Pour apple sauce into pan, spreading evenly. Sprinkle with cinnamon.

2. In large bowl, beat egg whites with electric mixer at high speed until foamy. Gradually add granulated sugar, beating until mixture is thick and light.

3. In small bowl, sift together flour, baking powder and salt. Fold into egg white mixture with vanilla. Gently pour batter over apple sauce mixture, spreading evenly.

4. Bake 15 to 18 minutes or until lightly browned. Cool on wire rack 5 minutes. Invert cake, apple sauce side up, onto clean, lint-free dish towel sprinkled with powdered sugar; peel off waxed paper. Trim edges of cake. Starting at narrow end, roll up cake. Place, seam side down, on serving plate. Cool completely. Sprinkle top with 1 tablespoon powdered sugar. Cut into 10 slices.

Makes 10 servings

Nutritional Information per Serving: *Calories: 120, Total Fat: ½ g, Cholesterol: 0 mg, Sodium: 100 mg*

Light Banana Cream Pie

1 package (1.9 ounces) sugar-free vanilla instant pudding and pie filling (four ½-cup servings)
2¾ cups low fat milk
4 ripe, medium DOLE® Bananas, sliced
1 (9-inch) ready-made graham cracker pie crust
1 firm, medium DOLE® Banana (optional)
Light frozen non-dairy whipped topping, thawed (optional)

• **Prepare** pudding as directed using 2¾ cups low fat milk. Stir in 4 sliced ripe bananas.

• **Spoon** banana mixture into pie crust. Place plastic wrap over pie, lightly pressing plastic to completely cover filling. Chill 1 hour or until filling is set. Remove plastic wrap.

• **Cut** firm banana into ½-inch slices. Garnish pie with whipped topping and banana slices.

Makes 8 servings

Prep Time: 10 minutes

Chill Time: 1 hour

Nutritional Information per Serving: *Calories: 199, Total Fat: 6 g, Cholesterol: 3 mg, Sodium: 242 mg*

Cherry Lattice Pie

2 packages (16 ounces each) frozen
    no-sugar-added pitted cherries
12¾ teaspoons EQUAL® For Recipes *or*
    42 packets EQUAL® sweetener *or*
    1¾ cup EQUAL® Spoonful™
4 teaspoons all-purpose flour
4 teaspoons cornstarch
¼ teaspoon ground nutmeg
5 to 7 drops red food color
    Reduced-Fat Pie Pastry (2 recipes for
    double crust, page 41) or favorite
    pastry for double crust 9-inch pie

• Thaw cherries completely in strainer set in bowl; reserve ¾ cup cherry juice. Mix Equal®, flour, cornstarch and nutmeg in small saucepan; stir in cherry juice and heat to boiling. Boil, stirring constantly, 1 minute. Remove from heat and stir in cherries; stir in food color.

• Roll half of pastry on floured surface into circle 1 inch larger than inverted 9-inch pie pan; ease pastry into pan. Pour cherry mixture into pastry. Roll remaining pastry on floured surface to ⅛-inch thickness; cut into 10 to 12 strips, ½ inch wide. Arrange pastry strips over filling and weave into lattice design. Trim ends of lattice strips; fold edge of lower crust over ends of lattice strips. Seal and flute edge.

• Bake in preheated 425°F oven until pastry is browned, 35 to 40 minutes. Cool on wire rack.   *Makes 8 servings*

Nutritional Information per Serving: *Calories: 330, Total Fat: 12 g, Cholesterol: 0 mg, Sodium: 269 mg*

Elegant Chocolate Angel Torte

⅓ cup HERSHEY'S Cocoa
1 package (about 15 ounces)
    "two-step" angel food cake mix
2 envelopes (1.3 ounces each)
    dry whipped topping mix
1 cup cold skim milk
1 teaspoon vanilla extract
1 cup strawberry purée*
    Strawberries

Mash 2 cups sliced fresh strawberries (or frozen berries, thawed) in blender or food processor. Cover; blend until smooth. Purée should measure 1 cup.

1. Move oven rack to lowest position. Sift cocoa over contents of cake flour packet; stir to blend. Proceed with mixing cake as directed on package. Bake and cool as directed for 10-inch tube pan. Carefully run knife along side of pan to loosen cake; remove from pan. Using serrated knife, slice cake horizontally into four layers.

2. Prepare whipped topping mix as directed on package, using 1 cup milk and 1 teaspoon vanilla. Blend in strawberry purée. Place bottom cake layer on serving plate; spread with ¼ of topping. Set next cake layer on top; spread with ¼ of topping. Continue layering cake and topping. Garnish with strawberries. Refrigerate until ready to serve. Slice cake with sharp serrated knife, cutting with gentle sawing motion. Cover; refrigerate leftover cake.

Makes about 16 servings

Prep Time: 30 minutes
Bake Time: 45 minutes
Cool Time: 2 hours

Nutritional Information per Serving (1 piece): *Calories: 150, Total Fat: 2 g, Cholesterol: 0 mg, Sodium: 210 mg*

Cherry Lattice Pie

Chocolate Swirled Cheesecake

Yogurt Cheese (recipe follows)
2 tablespoons graham cracker crumbs
1 package (8 ounces) Neufchâtel cheese (⅓ less fat cream cheese), softened
1½ teaspoons vanilla extract
¾ cup sugar
1 tablespoon cornstarch
1 container (8 ounces) liquid egg substitute
¼ cup HERSHEY'S Cocoa
¼ teaspoon almond extract

Prepare Yogurt Cheese. Heat oven to 325°F. Spray bottom of 8- or 9-inch springform pan with vegetable cooking spray. Sprinkle graham cracker crumbs on bottom of pan. In large mixer bowl, beat Yogurt Cheese, Neufchâtel cheese and vanilla on medium speed of electric mixer until smooth. Add sugar and cornstarch; beat just until well blended. Gradually add egg substitute, beating on low speed until blended. Transfer 1½ cups batter to medium bowl; add cocoa. Beat until well blended. Stir almond extract into vanilla batter. Alternately spoon vanilla and chocolate batters into prepared pan. With knife or metal spatula, cut through batters for marble effect.

Bake 35 minutes for 8-inch pan, 40 minutes for 9-inch pan or until edge is set. With knife, loosen cheesecake from side of pan. Cool completely in pan on wire rack. Cover; refrigerate at least 6 hours before serving. Just before serving, remove side of pan. Garnish as desired. Cover; refrigerate leftover cheesecake. *Makes 16 servings*

Yogurt Cheese: Use one 16-ounce container plain lowfat yogurt, no gelatin added. Line non-rusting colander or sieve with large piece of double thickness cheesecloth or large coffee filter; place colander over deep bowl. Spoon yogurt into prepared colander; cover with plastic wrap. Refrigerate until liquid no longer drains from yogurt, about 24 hours. Remove yogurt from cheesecloth and place in separate bowl; discard liquid.

Nutritional Information per Serving: *Calories 110, Total Fat 4 g, Cholesterol 15 mg, Sodium 100 mg*

Orange-Chocolate Bliss

1 (12.2-ounce) package low-fat devil's food cake mix plus ingredients to prepare cake
1 tablespoon grated orange peel
1 container (8 ounces) frozen whipped topping, thawed
2 tablespoons orange juice concentrate, thawed

1. Preheat oven to 350°F. Grease and flour 13×9×2-inch pan.

2. Combine cake mix and orange peel. Bake cake according to package directions.

3. Stir together whipped topping and orange juice concentrate in medium bowl until well blended. Cut cake into individual slices. Dollop each slice with topping.
Makes 16 servings

Nutritional Information per Serving: *Calories: 193, Total Fat: 7 g, Cholesterol: 52 mg Sodium: 271 mg,*

Raisin-Streusel Coffee Cake

1½ cups all-purpose flour
2 teaspoons baking powder
¼ teaspoon baking soda
¼ teaspoon salt
¾ cup granulated sugar
2 tablespoons margarine, softened
¾ cup nonfat sour cream
1 egg
1 teaspoon vanilla extract
½ cup MOTT'S® Chunky Apple Sauce
⅓ cup firmly packed light brown sugar
¼ cup raisins
2 tablespoons crunchy nut-like cereal nuggets

1. Preheat oven to 350°F. Spray 9-inch round cake pan with nonstick cooking spray.

2. In small bowl, combine flour, baking powder, baking soda and salt.

3. In large bowl, beat granulated sugar and margarine with electric mixer at medium speed until blended. Whisk in sour cream, egg and vanilla. Gently mix in apple sauce.

4. Add flour mixture to apple sauce mixture; stir until well blended. Pour batter into prepared pan.

5. In small bowl, combine brown sugar, raisins and cereal. Sprinkle over batter.

6. Bake 50 minutes or until toothpick inserted in center comes out clean. Cool 15 minutes on wire rack. Serve warm or cool completely. Cut into 14 slices.

Makes 14 servings

Nutritional Information per Serving: *Calories: 160, Total Fat: 2 g, Cholesterol: 15 mg, Sodium: 150 mg*

Angel Food Cake with Pineapple Sauce

1 can (20 ounces) DOLE® Crushed Pineapple, undrained
2 tablespoons sugar
1 tablespoon orange marmalade, peach or apricot fruit spread
1 tablespoon cornstarch
1 prepared angel food cake

• Combine undrained pineapple, sugar, orange marmalade and cornstarch in small saucepan. Bring to boil. Reduce heat to low; cook 2 minutes, stirring constantly, or until sauce thickens. Cool slightly. Sauce can be served warm or chilled.

• Cut angel food cake into 12 slices. To serve, spoon sauce over each slice.

Makes 12 servings

Prep Time: 10 minutes

Cook Time: 5 minutes

Nutritional Information per Serving: *Calories: 116, Total Fat: 0 g, Cholesterol: 0 mg, Sodium: 213 mg*

Mom's Lemon Meringue Pie

Reduced-Fat Pie Pastry (page 41)
or favorite pastry for 9-inch pie
2¼ **cups water**
½ **cup lemon juice**
10¾ **teaspoons EQUAL® For Recipes** *or*
36 packets EQUAL® sweetener *or*
1½ **cups EQUAL® Spoonful™**
⅓ **cup plus 2 tablespoons cornstarch**
2 **eggs**
2 **egg whites**
2 **tablespoons margarine**
1 **to 2 drops yellow food color**
(optional)
3 **egg whites**
¼ **teaspoon cream of tartar**
3½ **teaspoons EQUAL® For Recipes** *or*
12 packets EQUAL® sweetener*

*EQUAL® Spoonful™ cannot be used in meringue recipes.

• Roll pastry on lightly floured surface into circle 1 inch larger than inverted 9-inch pie pan. Ease pastry into pan; trim and flute edge. Pierce bottom and side of pastry with fork. Bake in preheated 425°F oven until pastry is browned, 10 to 15 minutes. Cool on wire rack.

• Mix water, lemon juice, 10¾ teaspoons Equal® For Recipes *or* 36 packets Equal® sweetener *or* 1½ cups Equal® Spoonful™ and cornstarch in medium saucepan. Heat to boiling over medium-high heat, stirring constantly; boil and stir 1 minute. Beat eggs and 2 egg whites in small bowl; stir in about half of hot cornstarch mixture. Stir egg mixture back into remaining cornstarch mixture in saucepan; cook and stir over low heat 1 minute. Remove from heat; add margarine, stirring until melted. Stir in food color, if desired. Pour mixture into baked pie shell.

• Beat 3 egg whites in medium bowl with electric mixer until foamy; add cream of tartar and beat to soft peaks. Gradually beat in 3½ teaspoons Equal® For Recipes *or* 12 packets Equal® sweetener, beating until stiff peaks form. Spread meringue over hot lemon filling, carefully sealing to edge of crust to prevent shrinking or weeping.

• Bake pie in preheated 425°F oven until meringue is browned, about 5 minutes. Cool completely on wire rack before cutting.

Makes 8 servings

Nutritional Information per Serving: *Calories: 233, Total Fat: 10 g, Cholesterol: 53 mg, Sodium: 223 mg*

Honey Pumpkin Pie

1 **can (16 ounces) solid-pack pumpkin**
1 **cup evaporated low-fat milk**
¾ **cup honey**
3 **eggs, slightly beaten**
2 **tablespoons all-purpose flour**
1 **teaspoon ground cinnamon**
½ **teaspoon ground ginger**
½ **teaspoon rum extract**
Pastry for single 9-inch pie crust

Combine all ingredients except pastry in large bowl; beat until well blended. Pour into pastry-lined 9-inch pie plate. Bake at 400°F 45 minutes or until knife inserted near center comes out clean.

Makes 8 servings

Nutritional Information per Serving: *Calories: 284, Total Fat: 9 g, Cholesterol: 82 mg, Sodium: 209 mg*

Favorite recipe from **National Honey Board**

Mom's Lemon Meringue Pie

Summer Fruit Tart

1¼ cups all-purpose flour
¼ teaspoon salt
⅓ cup shortening
3 to 4 tablespoons cold water
¼ cup plain nonfat yogurt
¼ cup reduced-fat dairy sour cream
½ teaspoon EQUAL® For Recipes *or*
    2 packets EQUAL® sweetener *or*
    4 teaspoons EQUAL® Spoonful™
¼ teaspoon almond extract
4 cups assorted fresh fruit
¾ cup pineapple juice
1 tablespoon lemon juice
2 teaspoons cornstarch
1 teaspoon EQUAL® For Recipes *or*
    3 packets EQUAL® sweetener *or*
    2 tablespoons EQUAL® Spoonful™

• Combine flour and salt; cut in shortening. Sprinkle water over mixture; toss with fork until moistened. Form into a ball.

• Roll pastry on lightly floured surface into 10- or 11-inch circle and place in 9- or 10-inch tart pan with removable bottom. Press pastry up side; trim excess. Prick with fork. Line with foil. Bake in preheated 450°F oven 8 minutes. Remove foil; bake until golden, 5 to 6 minutes. Cool on wire rack.

• Combine yogurt, sour cream, ½ teaspoon Equal® For Recipes *or* 2 packets Equal® sweetener *or* 4 teaspoons Equal® Spoonful™ and almond extract. Spread over cooled crust. Arrange fruit on top.

• Combine pineapple juice, lemon juice and cornstarch in small saucepan. Cook and stir until thickened and bubbly. Cook and stir 2 minutes more. Remove from heat; stir in 1 teaspoon Equal® For Recipes *or* 3 packets Equal® sweetener *or* 2 tablespoons Equal® Spoonful™. Cool. Spoon over fruit; cover and chill. *Makes 10 servings*

Nutritional Information per Serving: *Calories: 166, Total Fat: 8 g, Cholesterol: 1 mg, Sodium: 65 mg*

Nectarine and Berry Pie

Reduced-Fat Pie Pastry (page 41)
    or favorite pastry for 9-inch pie
5 cups sliced nectarines (about
    5 medium)
1 cup raspberries or sliced strawberries
1 cup fresh or frozen blueberries,
    partially thawed
2 teaspoons lemon juice
3 tablespoons cornstarch
7¼ teaspoons EQUAL® For Recipes *or*
    24 packets EQUAL® sweetener *or*
    1 cup EQUAL® Spoonful™
1 teaspoon grated lemon peel
¼ teaspoon ground allspice

• Roll pastry on floured surface into 12-inch circle; transfer to ungreased cookie sheet.

• Toss nectarines and berries with lemon juice in large bowl; sprinkle fruit with combined cornstarch, Equal®, lemon peel and allspice and toss to coat. Arrange fruit over pastry, leaving 2-inch border around edge of pastry. Bring edge of pastry toward center, overlapping as necessary. Bake pie in preheated 425°F oven until pastry is golden and fruit is tender, 35 to 40 minutes. Cool on wire rack. *Makes 8 servings*

Nutritional Information per Serving: *Calories: 216, Total Fat: 7 g, Cholesterol: 0 mg, Sodium: 138 mg*

Summer Fruit Tart

Marble Cheesecake

CRUMB CRUST

12 cinnamon graham crackers
(5×2½-inch)
¼ cup sugar
¼ teaspoon ground cinnamon
6 tablespoons unsalted butter, at room
temperature
2 tablespoons cold water

MARBLE CHEESE FILLING

¾ cup 2% low fat milk
4 cups (1 pound) shredded ALPINE
LACE® Reduced Sodium Muenster
Cheese
¾ cup sugar
2 tablespoons all-purpose flour
1 cup egg substitute *or* 4 large eggs,
slightly beaten
⅓ cup mini semi-sweet chocolate chips,
melted
1 teaspoon vanilla extract

SOUR CREAM TOPPING

2 cups fat free sour cream
2 tablespoons sugar
1 teaspoon vanilla extract
½ pint fresh raspberries

1. To make the Crumb Crust: Preheat the
oven to 350°F. Spray a 10-inch springform
pan with nonstick cooking spray. In a food
processor, place the graham crackers, the
¼ cup sugar and the cinnamon; process for
1 minute or until finely ground. Add the
butter and water; process 30 seconds more
or until moistened. Press onto the bottom
and 1½ inches up the side of the pan.

2. To make the Marble Cheese Filling: In a
small saucepan, bring the milk to a boil over
medium-high heat. In a food processor,
process the cheese, the ¾ cup sugar, and
the flour for 1 minute or until coarsely
ground. With the motor running, add the
hot milk through the feed tube, then the
egg substitute (or the 4 whole eggs).
Process 1 minute or until smooth and pour
into a large bowl. For Recipes out ½ cup of
the batter; stir in the melted chips and
vanilla. Set aside.

3. Pour the white batter into the crust.
Randomly spoon the chocolate batter on
top. Gently cut through the batter to make
chocolate swirls. Bake on the middle rack of
the oven for 35 minutes. Transfer cake in
pan to a rack to cool for 5 minutes.

4. While cake bakes, make the Sour Cream
Topping: In a small bowl, stir together sour
cream, the 2 tablespoons sugar and the
vanilla. Carefully spread topping evenly on
top of cake.

5. Return cake to the oven and bake 10
minutes more or until topping is set. Cool
cake in pan. Chill for 1 hour, garnish with
the raspberries and chill 1 hour more or
overnight. If you wish, decorate with fresh
mint leaves before serving.

Makes 24 servings

Nutritional Information per Serving: *Calories: 183,
Total Fat: 11 g, Cholesterol: 26 mg*

Marble Cheesecake

Rocky Road Cake

1¾ cups all-purpose flour
⅓ cup unsweetened cocoa powder
2 teaspoons baking powder
1 teaspoon baking soda
½ teaspoon salt
1 cup granulated sugar
¾ cup MOTT'S® Natural Apple Sauce
½ cup skim milk
4 egg whites
1 teaspoon vanilla extract
Powdered sugar
¾ cup marshmallow topping
½ cup frozen light nondairy whipped
topping, thawed
2 tablespoons chopped unsalted
peanuts
Fresh red currants (optional)
Mint leaves (optional)

1. Preheat oven to 350°F. Line 15½×10½-inch jelly-roll pan with waxed paper.

2. In medium bowl, sift together flour, cocoa, baking powder, baking soda and salt.

3. In large bowl, whisk together granulated sugar, apple sauce, milk, egg whites and vanilla.

4. Add flour mixture to apple sauce mixture; stir until well blended. Pour batter into prepared pan.

5. Bake 12 to 15 minutes or until top springs back when lightly touched. Immediately invert onto clean, lint-free dish towel sprinkled with powdered sugar; peel off waxed paper. Trim edges of cake. Starting at narrow end, roll up cake and towel together. Cool completely on wire rack.

6. In small bowl, whisk marshmallow topping until softened. Gently fold in whipped topping.

7. Unroll cake; spread with marshmallow mixture to within ½ inch of edges of cake. Sprinkle peanuts over marshmallow mixture. Reroll cake; place, seam side down, on serving plate. Cover; refrigerate 1 hour before slicing. Sprinkle with powdered sugar and garnish with currants and mint leaves, if desired, just before serving. Cut into 14 slices. Refrigerate leftovers.

Makes 14 servings

Nutritional Information per Serving: *Calories: 190, Total Fat: ½ g, Cholesterol: 0 mg, Sodium: 210 mg*

Cheesecake for One

¼ cup cold water
1 envelope unflavored gelatin
¼ cup ground almonds
1 tablespoon margarine, melted
12 ounces light cream cheese
¾ cup fat-free (skim) milk
½ cup sugar
¼ teaspoon vanilla extract
3 cups peeled mango slices, puréed

1. Combine cold water and gelatin in small saucepan; stir over low heat until dissolved.

2. Combine almonds and margarine in small bowl. Press mixture evenly onto bottoms of 12 paper-lined baking cups.

3. Beat together cream cheese, milk, sugar and vanilla in large mixing bowl at medium speed with electric mixer until well blended. Stir in gelatin mixture. Pour into baking cups; freeze until firm.

4. Remove cheesecakes from freezer 10 minutes before serving. Spoon mango purée onto serving plates. Invert cheesecakes onto plates. *Makes 12 servings*

Nutritional Information per Serving: *Calories: 175, Total Fat: 10 g, Cholesterol: 11 mg, Sodium: 180 mg*

Rocky Road Cake

More Desserts

Lemon Raspberry Tiramisu

2 packages (8 ounces each) fat-free
    cream cheese, softened
6 packages artificial sweetener or
    equivalent of ¼ cup sugar
1 teaspoon vanilla
⅓ cup water
1 package (0.3 ounce) sugar-free
    lemon-flavored gelatin
2 cups thawed fat-free nondairy
    whipped topping
½ cup all-fruit red raspberry preserves
¼ cup water
2 tablespoons marsala wine
2 packages (3 ounces each) ladyfingers
1 pint fresh raspberries or frozen
    unsweetened raspberries, thawed

1. Combine cream cheese, artificial sweetener and vanilla in large bowl. Beat with electric mixer at high speed until smooth; set aside.

2. Combine water and gelatin in small microwavable bowl; microwave at HIGH 30 seconds to 1 minute or until water is boiling and gelatin is dissolved. Cool slightly.

3. Add gelatin mixture to cheese mixture; beat 1 minute. Add whipped topping; beat 1 minute more, scraping side of bowl. Set aside.

4. Whisk together preserves, water and marsala in small bowl until well blended. Reserve 2 tablespoons preserves mixture; set aside. Spread ⅓ cup preserves mixture evenly over bottom of 11×7-inch glass baking dish.

5. Split ladyfingers in half; place half on bottom of baking dish. Spread ½ of cheese mixture evenly over ladyfingers; sprinkle 1 cup raspberries evenly over cheese mixture. Top with remaining ladyfingers; spread remaining preserves mixture over ladyfingers. Top with remaining cheese mixture. Cover; refrigerate at least 2 hours. Sprinkle with remaining raspberries and drizzle with reserved 2 tablespoons preserves mixture before serving. *Makes 12 servings*

Nutritional Information per Serving: *Calories: 158, Total Fat: 1 g, Cholesterol: 52 mg, Sodium: 272 mg*

Lemon Raspberry Tiramisu

Lots O'Apple Pizza

    2 cups MOTT'S® Natural Apple Sauce
    1 teaspoon vanilla extract
    ¾ teaspoon active dry yeast
    ½ teaspoon granulated sugar
    ½ cup plus 1 tablespoon warm water
        (105° to 115°F)
    1¼ cups all-purpose flour
    ½ teaspoon salt
    ⅔ cup raisins
    2 cups unpeeled, thinly sliced tart
        apples (about 2 medium)
        Additional raisins (optional)
    2 tablespoons powdered sugar

1. In medium saucepan, combine apple sauce and vanilla. Cook over medium heat, stirring occasionally, until reduced by half. Set aside.

2. In small bowl, sprinkle yeast and granulated sugar over warm water; stir until yeast dissolves. Let stand 5 minutes or until mixture is bubbly.

3. In medium bowl, combine flour and salt. Make well in center of mixture.

4. Pour yeast mixture into flour mixture; stir until soft dough forms. Let rise 5 minutes. Turn out dough onto floured surface; flatten slightly. Knead 5 to 10 minutes or until smooth and elastic. Shape dough into ball; place dough in large bowl sprayed with nonstick cooking spray. Turn dough over so that top is greased. Cover with towel; let rise in warm place 45 minutes to 1 hour or until doubled in bulk.

5. Punch down dough; let rise about 30 minutes in warm place or until doubled in bulk.

6. Preheat oven to 450°F. Spray 12-inch pizza pan with nonstick cooking spray.

7. Spread dough or roll with lightly floured rolling pin into 12-inch circle. Place in prepared pan. Spread half of apple sauce mixture over dough to within ½ inch of edge. Sprinkle with ⅔ cup raisins. Arrange apple slices over pizza, covering raisins. Spread remaining apple sauce mixture over apple slices.

8. Bake 15 to 20 minutes or until edge of crust is lightly browned. Cool completely on wire rack. Garnish with additional raisins, if desired. Sprinkle with powdered sugar. Cut into 12 wedges.   *Makes 12 servings*

Note: Substitute prepared pizza dough for homemade dough, if desired.

Nutritional Information per Serving: *Calories: 110, Total Fat: 1 g, Cholesterol: 0 mg, Sodium: 90 mg*

Black Cherry Freeze

    1 cup boiling water
    1 package (4-serving size) black
        cherry-flavored sugar-free gelatin
    ½ cup diet cherry soda
    1 container (8 ounces) plain low-fat
        yogurt
    2 cups thawed frozen whipped
        topping

1. Combine boiling water and gelatin; stir until gelatin dissolves. Add soda. Stir in yogurt until well blended and smooth. Fold in whipped topping; pour into 9-inch square baking pan.

2. Freeze until firm, about 6 hours or overnight.   *Makes 7 (½-cup) servings*

Nutritional Information per Serving: *Calories: 80, Total Fat: 4 g, Cholesterol: 5 mg, Sodium: 60 mg*

Lots O'Apple Pizza

Fruit Baked Apples

3½ teaspoons EQUAL® For Recipes or
    12 packets EQUAL® sweetener or
    ½ cup EQUAL® Spoonful™
1 tablespoon cornstarch
    Pinch ground cinnamon
    Pinch ground nutmeg
2 cups apple cider or juice
1 package (6 ounces) dried mixed fruit, chopped
1 tablespoon margarine
8 tart baking apples

• Combine Equal®, cornstarch, cinnamon and nutmeg in medium saucepan; stir in cider. Add dried fruit; heat to boiling. Reduce heat and simmer, uncovered, until fruit is tender and cider mixture is reduced to about 1 cup, 10 to 15 minutes. Add margarine and stir until melted.

• Remove cores from apples, cutting to, but not through, bottoms. Peel 1 inch around tops. Place apples in greased baking pan. Fill centers with fruit; spoon remaining cider mixture over apples.

• Bake, uncovered, in preheated 350°F oven until fork-tender, about 45 minutes.

Makes 8 servings

Nutritional Information per Serving: *Calories: 176, Total Fat: 2 g, Cholesterol: 0 mg, Sodium: 22 mg*

Cheese-Filled Poached Pears

1½ quarts cranberry-raspberry juice cocktail
2 ripe Bartlett pears with stems, peeled
2 tablespoons Neufchâtel cheese
2 teaspoons crumbled Gorgonzola cheese
1 tablespoon chopped walnuts

1. Bring juice to a boil in medium saucepan over high heat. Add pears; reduce heat to medium-low. Simmer 15 minutes or until pears are tender, turning occasionally. Remove pears from saucepan; discard liquid. Let stand 10 minutes or until cool enough to handle.

2. Combine cheeses in small bowl until well blended. Cut thin slice off bottom of each pear so that pears stand evenly. Cut pears lengthwise in half, leaving stems intact. Scoop out seeds and membranes to form small hole in each pear half. Fill holes with cheese mixture; press halves together. Place nuts in large bowl; roll pears in nuts to coat. Cover; refrigerate until ready to serve.

Makes 2 servings

Nutritional Information per Serving: *Calories: 240, Total Fat: 7 g, Cholesterol: 13 mg, Sodium: 98 mg*

Honey-Caramelized Bananas and Oranges

2 large bananas
1 orange, peeled and sliced
¼ cup honey
2 tablespoons chopped walnuts
3 tablespoons brandy (optional)

Peel and cut bananas in half lengthwise; place in small flameproof dish with orange slices. Drizzle with honey; sprinkle with walnuts. On top rack of preheated broiler, broil fruit about 5 minutes or until heated but not burnt. Remove from broiler. If desired, pour brandy over top and flame.

Makes 2 servings

Nutritional Information per Serving: *Calories: 362, Total Fat: 4 g, Cholesterol: 0 mg, Sodium: 3 mg*

Favorite recipe from **National Honey Board**

Fruit Baked Apples

Fresh Fruit with Peach Glaze

2 cups DOLE® Orange Peach Mango, Pineapple Orange, Pine-Orange-Banana or Country Raspberry Juice
3 tablespoons sugar
1 tablespoon cornstarch
1 tablespoon lemon juice
½ teaspoon grated lemon peel
8 cups cut-up fresh fruit such as DOLE® Fresh Pineapple, Bananas, Strawberries, Red or Green Seedless Grapes, Cantaloupe, Oranges, Peaches, Nectarines or Kiwi

• Combine peach juice, sugar, cornstarch, lemon juice and lemon peel in medium saucepan.

• Cook and stir over medium-high heat 5 minutes or until mixture comes to boil. Reduce heat to low; cook 2 minutes or until slightly thickened. Cool slightly. Sauce can be served warm or chilled.

• Arrange fruit in dessert dishes. Spoon glaze over fruit. Refrigerate any leftovers in air-tight container.   *Makes 8 servings*

Prep Time: 5 minutes
Cook Time: 5 minutes

Nutritional Information per Serving: *Calories: 125, Total Fat: 0 g, Cholesterol: 0 mg, Sodium: 19 mg*

Apple Clafouti

2 jars (23 ounces each) MOTT'S® Chunky Apple Sauce
⅔ cup raisins
1 teaspoon ground cinnamon
1 cup all-purpose flour
1 teaspoon baking powder
½ teaspoon salt
3 egg whites
¼ cup low fat buttermilk
¼ cup honey
  Powdered sugar

1. Preheat oven to 400°F. Spray two 9-inch glass pie plates with nonstick cooking spray.

2. In large bowl, combine apple sauce, raisins and cinnamon.

3. In small bowl, combine flour, baking powder and salt.

4. In medium bowl, whisk together egg whites, buttermilk and honey until slightly frothy.

5. Add flour mixture to egg white mixture; whisk until well blended. Pour ½ cup batter into each prepared pie plate.

6. Bake 4 to 5 minutes or until lightly browned. Pour half of apple sauce mixture over each baked layer. Spoon remaining batter over apple sauce mixture; spread evenly.

7. *Reduce oven temperature to 350°F.* Bake 15 to 20 minutes or until tops are puffy and lightly browned.

8. Cool completely on wire racks; sprinkle tops with powdered sugar. Slice each dessert into 6 wedges. Refrigerate leftovers.
        Makes 12 servings

Nutritional Information per Serving: *Calories: 180, Total Fat: ½ g, Cholesterol: 0 mg, Sodium: 135 mg*

Fresh Fruit with Peach Glaze

Caramelized Peaches & Cream

2 pounds (about 8 medium) sliced peeled peaches, or thawed and well-drained unsweetened frozen peaches
2 tablespoons bourbon
¾ cup reduced-fat sour cream
½ teaspoon ground cinnamon
¼ teaspoon ground nutmeg
¾ cup packed light brown sugar
8 slices (1½ ounces each) angel food cake, cut into cubes

1. Toss peaches with bourbon in shallow ovenproof 1½-quart casserole or 11×7-inch glass baking dish. Press down into even layer.

2. Combine sour cream, cinnamon and nutmeg in small bowl; mix well. Spoon mixture evenly over peaches. (Mixture may be covered and refrigerated up to 2 hours before cooking time.)

3. Preheat broiler. Sprinkle brown sugar evenly over sour cream mixture to cover. Broil 4 to 5 inches from heat, 3 to 5 minutes or until brown sugar is melted and bubbly. (Watch closely after 3 minutes so that sugar does not burn.)

4. Spoon immediately over angel food cake.

Makes 10 servings

Nutritional Information per Serving: *Calories: 215, Total Fat: 1 g, Cholesterol: 6 mg, Sodium: 272 mg*

Spiced Grilled Bananas

3 large ripe firm bananas
¼ cup golden raisins
3 tablespoons packed brown sugar
½ teaspoon ground cinnamon
¼ teaspoon ground cardamom
¼ teaspoon ground nutmeg
2 tablespoons margarine, cut into 8 pieces
1 tablespoon fresh lime juice
Vanilla low-fat frozen yogurt (optional)
Additional fresh lime juice (optional)

1. Spray grill-proof 9-inch pie plate with nonstick cooking spray. Prepare coals for grilling. Cut bananas diagonally into ½-inch-thick slices. Arrange, overlapping, in prepared pie plate. Sprinkle with raisins.

2. Combine sugar, cinnamon, cardamom and nutmeg in small bowl; sprinkle over bananas and raisins and dot with margarine. Cover pie plate tightly with foil. Place on grid and grill on covered grill over low coals 10 to 15 minutes or until bananas are hot and tender. Carefully remove foil and sprinkle with 1 tablespoon lime juice. Serve over low-fat frozen yogurt and sprinkle with additional lime juice, if desired.

Makes 4 servings

Nutritional Information per Serving: *Calories: 202, Total Fat: 6 g, Cholesterol: 0 mg, Sodium: 72 mg*

Caramelized Peaches & Cream

Grandma's Apple Crisp

¾ cup apple juice
3½ teaspoons EQUAL® For Recipes *or*
    12 packets EQUAL® sweetener *or*
    ½ cup EQUAL® Spoonful™
1 tablespoon cornstarch
1 teaspoon grated lemon peel
4 cups sliced peeled apples
    Crispy Topping (recipe follows)

• Combine apple juice, Equal®, cornstarch and lemon peel in medium saucepan; add apples and heat to boiling. Reduce heat and simmer, uncovered, until juice is thickened and apples begin to lose their crispness, about 5 minutes.

• Arrange apples in 8-inch square baking pan; sprinkle Crispy Topping over apples. Bake in preheated 400°F oven until topping is browned and apples are tender, about 25 minutes. Serve warm.   *Makes 6 servings*

Crispy Topping

¼ cup all-purpose flour
2½ teaspoons EQUAL® For Recipes *or*
    8 packets EQUAL® sweetener *or*
    ⅓ cup EQUAL® Spoonful™
1 teaspoon ground cinnamon
½ teaspoon ground nutmeg
3 dashes ground allspice
4 tablespoons cold margarine, cut into pieces
¼ cup uncooked quick-cooking oats
¼ cup unsweetened flaked coconut*

Unsweetened coconut can be purchased in health food stores.

• Combine flour, Equal® and spices in small bowl; cut in margarine with pastry blender until mixture resembles coarse crumbs. Stir in oats and coconut.

Nutritional Information per Serving: *Calories: 196, Total Fat: 10 g, Cholesterol: 0 mg, Sodium: 91 mg*

Baked Apple Crisp

8 cups unpeeled, thinly sliced apples (about 8 medium)
2 tablespoons granulated sugar
1½ tablespoons lemon juice
4 teaspoons ground cinnamon, divided
1½ cups MOTT'S® Natural Apple Sauce
1 cup uncooked rolled oats
½ cup firmly packed light brown sugar
⅓ cup all-purpose flour
⅓ cup evaporated skimmed milk
¼ cup nonfat dry milk powder
1 cup nonfat vanilla yogurt

1. Preheat oven to 350°F. Spray 2-quart casserole with nonstick cooking spray.

2. In large bowl, toss apple slices with granulated sugar, lemon juice and 2 teaspoons cinnamon. Spoon into prepared dish. Spread apple sauce evenly over apple mixture.

3. In medium bowl, combine oats, brown sugar, flour, evaporated milk, dry milk powder and remaining 2 teaspoons cinnamon. Spread over apple sauce.

4. Bake 35 to 40 minutes or until lightly browned and bubbly. Cool slightly; serve warm. Top each serving with dollop of yogurt.   *Makes 12 servings*

Nutritional Information per Serving: *Calories: 185, Total Fat: 2 g, Cholesterol: 0 mg, Sodium: 35 mg*

Grandma's Apple Crisp

Smucker's® Peachy Pear Crumble

½ cup SMUCKER'S® Peach Preserves
¼ cup lemon juice
¼ teaspoon ground ginger
 6 pears, peeled, cored and sliced
¼ cup all-purpose flour
¼ cup oatmeal
⅛ teaspoon salt
¼ teaspoon ground cinnamon
 1 tablespoon margarine
 1 tablespoon brown sugar
 2 tablespoon milk
 6 teaspoons low-fat frozen yogurt or non-fat sour cream (optional)

Preheat oven to 375°F. Place Smucker's® Peach Preserves, lemon juice and ginger in saucepan over medium high heat. Simmer until preserves are liquefied. Add pear slices and simmer 5 minutes.

While pears are simmering, combine flour, oatmeal, brown sugar and cinnamon in small bowl. Blend in margarine until mixture resembles rough meal. Add milk and loosely combine until just blended.

Pour pear mixture into 8-inch square baking pan. Sprinkle crumble topping evenly over surface of pear mixture. Place pan in preheated oven and bake 25 to 30 minutes or until top is lightly browned and bubbling.

Serve warm plain or with several tablespoons low-fat frozen yogurt, if desired.

Makes 6 servings

Note: If time is of the essence, substitute pear halves packaged in light syrup for the fresh pears in this recipe. Bake 15 minutes rather than 25 to 30. Top the pear mixture with a few tablespoons of your favorite granola for a speedy topping.

Nutritional Information per Serving: *Calories: 197, Total Fat: 3 g, Cholesterol: trace, Sodium: 84 mg*

Tropical Bread Pudding with Piña Colada Sauce

BREAD PUDDING

 6 cups cubed day-old French bread
 1 cup skim milk
 1 cup frozen orange-pineapple-banana juice concentrate, thawed
½ cup cholesterol:-free egg substitute
 2 teaspoons vanilla
½ teaspoon butter-flavored extract
 1 can (8 ounces) crushed pineapple in juice, undrained
½ cup golden raisins

PIÑA COLADA SAUCE

¾ cup all-fruit pineapple preserves
⅓ cup shredded unsweetened coconut, toasted
 1 teaspoon rum *or* ⅛ teaspoon rum extract

1. To prepare bread pudding, preheat oven to 350°F. Spray 11×7-inch glass baking dish with nonstick cooking spray. Place cubed bread in large bowl; set aside.

2. Combine milk, juice concentrate, egg substitute, vanilla and butter-flavored extract in another large bowl; mix until smooth. Drain pineapple; reserve juice. Add milk mixture, pineapple and raisins to bread; gently mix with large spoon. Spoon bread mixture evenly into prepared baking dish and flatten slightly; bake, uncovered, 40 minutes. Cool slightly.

3. To prepare Piña Colada Sauce, add water to reserved pineapple juice to equal ¼ cup. Combine juice, preserves, coconut and rum in microwavable bowl. Microwave at HIGH 2 to 3 minutes or until sauce is hot and bubbling; cool to room temperature.

4. Divide pudding among 8 plates; top each serving with 2 tablespoons Piña Colada Sauce. *Makes 8 servings*

Nutritional Information per Serving: *Calories: 280, Total Fat: 2 g, Cholesterol: 1 mg, Sodium: 178 mg*

Low-Sugar Chocolate Mint Mousse

1 package (1 ounce) sugar-free
   whipped topping mix
½ cup cold water
2 envelopes unflavored gelatin
1 cup boiling water
1 cup instant nonfat dry milk powder
⅓ cup HERSHEY'S Cocoa
   Granulated sugar substitute to equal
   ⅔ cup sugar
1 tablespoon vanilla extract
½ teaspoon mint extract
   Dash salt
2 cups ice cubes *or* 1½ cups crushed ice
   Additional HERSHEY'S Cocoa
   (optional)

Prepare whipped topping mix according to package directions; set aside.

Pour cold water into blender container. Sprinkle gelatin over water; let stand 3 to 4 minutes. Add boiling water. Cover; blend on low speed, occasionally scraping sides of blender with rubber scraper, until gelatin is completely dissolved, about 2 minutes. Add dry milk powder, ⅓ cup cocoa, sugar substitute, vanilla and mint extracts and salt. Cover; blend well. Add ice cubes. Cover; blend on high speed until mixture is smooth.

Pour mixture into large bowl. Fold in 1 cup whipped topping; reserve remaining topping for garnish. Spoon mousse into parfait or wine glasses. Refrigerate until set, about 45 minutes. Garnish with remaining topping. Sift additional cocoa over top, if desired.   *Makes 8 servings*

Nutritional Information per Serving: *Calories: 110, Total Fat: 3 g, Cholesterol: 0 mg, Sodium: 85 mg*

Fudge Sundae Pudding

1 cup all-purpose flour
⅔ cup plus ¼ cup granulated sugar,
   divided
4 tablespoons unsweetened cocoa
   powder, divided
2 teaspoons baking powder
½ teaspoon salt
½ cup skim milk
1 teaspoon vanilla extract
½ cup firmly packed light brown sugar
1 cup water
1 cup MOTT'S® Natural Apple Sauce
   Frozen low fat vanilla yogurt or
   frozen light nondairy whipped
   topping, thawed (optional)

1. Preheat oven to 350°F. Spray 8-inch square baking pan with nonstick cooking spray.

2. In medium bowl, combine flour, ⅔ cup granulated sugar, 2 tablespoons cocoa, baking powder and salt. Add milk and vanilla; mix well. Spread batter into prepared pan.

3. In small bowl, combine brown sugar, remaining ¼ cup granulated sugar and 2 tablespoons cocoa. Sprinkle evenly over batter.

4. Combine water and apple sauce in small saucepan. Bring to a boil over high heat. Pour over batter. *Do not stir.*

5. Bake 35 to 40 minutes or until center is almost set. Serve immediately with frozen yogurt or whipped topping, if desired.
           Makes 10 servings

Nutritional Information per Serving: *Calories: 180, Total Fat: 1 g, Cholesterol: 0 mg, Sodium: 170 mg*

Chocolate-Filled Meringue Shells with Strawberry Sauce

   2 egg whites
   ¼ teaspoon cream of tartar
      Dash salt
   ¾ cup sugar
   ¼ teaspoon vanilla extract
      Chocolate Filling (recipe follows)
   1 package (10 ounces) frozen
         strawberries in syrup, thawed

Heat oven to 275°F. Line 10 muffin cups (2½ inches in diameter) with paper bake cups. In small mixer bowl, beat egg whites with cream of tartar and salt at high speed of electric mixer until soft peaks form. Beat in sugar, 1 tablespoon at a time, beating well after each addition until stiff peaks hold their shape, sugar is dissolved and mixture is glossy. Fold in vanilla. Spoon about 3 tablespoons mixture in each muffin cup. Using back of spoon or small spatula, push mixture up sides of muffin cups to form well in center.

Bake 1 hour or until meringues turn delicate cream color and feel dry to the touch. Cool in pan on wire rack. Before serving, carefully remove paper from shells. For each serving, spoon 1 heaping tablespoonful Chocolate Filling into meringue shell. In blender container, place strawberries with syrup. Cover; blend until smooth. Spoon over filled shells. Garnish as desired. To store leftover unfilled shells, peel paper bake cups from remaining shells; store shells loosely covered at room temperature.   *Makes 10 servings*

Chocolate Filling: In small mixer bowl, beat 4 ounces (½ of 8-ounce package) softened Neufchâtel cheese (light cream cheese) and ¼ cup **HERSHEY'S** Cocoa on medium speed of electric mixer until blended. Gradually add ¾ cup powdered sugar, beating until well blended. Fold in 1 cup frozen light non-dairy whipped topping, thawed.

Nutritional Information per Serving: *Calories: 170, Total Fat: 4 g, Cholesterol: 10 mg, Sodium: 95 mg*

Microwave Chocolate Pudding

   ⅓ cup sugar
   ¼ cup **HERSHEY'S** Cocoa
   2 tablespoons cornstarch
   1½ cups 2% low-fat milk
   1 teaspoon vanilla
   ⅛ teaspoon ground cinnamon
         (optional)
      Assorted small candies (optional)

1. Combine sugar, cocoa and cornstarch in medium microwavable bowl or 1-quart glass measure. Gradually add milk, stirring with wire wisk until well blended.

2. Microwave at HIGH 2 minutes; stir. Microwave at MEDIUM-HIGH (70%) 3½ to 4½ minutes or until thickened, stirring every 1½ minutes.

3. Stir in vanilla and cinnamon. Let stand at least 5 minutes before serving, stirring occasionally to prevent skin from forming. Serve warm or chilled. Garnish with candies just before serving, if desired.
     Makes 4 servings

Nutritional Information per Serving: *Calories: 139, Total Fat: 2 g, Cholesterol: 7 mg, Sodium: 50 mg*

Chocolate-Filled Meringue Shells with Strawberry Sauce

Maple Caramel Bread Pudding

    8 slices cinnamon raisin bread
    2 whole eggs
    1 egg white
    ⅓ cup sugar
    1½ cups 2% low-fat milk
    ½ cup maple syrup
    ½ teaspoon ground cinnamon
    ¼ teaspoon salt
    ¼ teaspoon ground nutmeg
    6 tablespoons fat-free caramel ice
        cream topping

1. Preheat oven to 350°F. Spray 8×8-inch baking dish with nonstick cooking spray. Cut bread into ¾-inch cubes; arrange in prepared dish.

2. Beat whole eggs, egg white and sugar in medium bowl. Beat in milk, syrup, cinnamon, salt and nutmeg; pour evenly over bread. Toss bread gently to coat.

3. Bake 45 minutes or until center is set. Transfer dish to wire cooling rack; let stand 20 minutes before serving. Serve warm with caramel topping. *Makes 8 servings*

Nutritional Information per Serving: *Calories: 235, Total Fat: 3 g, Cholesterol: 57 mg, Sodium: 228 mg*

Blueberry Bread Pudding with Caramel Sauce

    8 slices white bread, cubed
    1 cup fresh or frozen blueberries
    2 cups skim milk
    1 cup EGG BEATERS® Healthy Real Egg
        Substitute
    ⅔ cup sugar
    1 teaspoon vanilla extract
    ¼ teaspoon ground cinnamon
        Caramel Sauce (recipe follows)

Place bread cubes on bottom of lightly greased 8×8×2-inch baking pan. Sprinkle with blueberries; set aside.

In large bowl, combine milk, Egg Beaters®, sugar, vanilla and cinnamon; pour over bread mixture. Set pan in larger pan filled with 1-inch depth hot water. Bake at 350°F for 1 hour or until knife inserted in center comes out clean. Serve warm with Caramel Sauce. *Makes 9 servings*

Prep Time: 20 minutes

Cook Time: 1 hour

Caramel Sauce: In small saucepan, over low heat, heat ¼ cup skim milk and 14 vanilla caramels until caramels are melted, stirring frequently.

Nutritional Information per Serving: *Calories: 210, Total Fat: 2 g, Cholesterol: 2 mg, Sodium: 227 mg*

Creamy Tapioca Pudding

    2 cups skim milk
    3 tablespoons quick-cooking tapioca
    1 egg
    ⅛ teaspoon salt
    3½ teaspoons EQUAL® For Recipes *or*
        12 packets EQUAL® sweetener *or*
        ½ cup EQUAL® Spoonful™
    1 to 2 teaspoons vanilla
        Ground cinnamon and nutmeg

• Combine milk, tapioca, egg and salt in medium saucepan. Let stand 5 minutes. Cook over medium-high heat, stirring constantly, until boiling. Remove from heat; stir in Equal® and vanilla.

• Spoon mixture into serving dishes; sprinkle lightly with cinnamon and nutmeg. Serve warm, or refrigerate and serve chilled. *Makes 4 (⅔-cup) servings*

Nutritional Information per Serving: *Calories: 101, Total Fat: 1 g, Cholesterol: 55 mg, Sodium: 146 mg*

Maple Caramel Bread Pudding

Rice Pudding

1¼ cups water, divided
½ cup uncooked long-grain rice
2 cups evaporated skimmed milk
½ cup granulated sugar
½ cup raisins
½ cup MOTT'S® Natural Apple Sauce
3 tablespoons cornstarch
1 teaspoon vanilla extract
    Brown sugar or nutmeg (optional)
    Fresh raspberries (optional)
    Orange peel strips (optional)

1. In medium saucepan, bring 1 cup water to a boil. Add rice. Reduce heat to low and simmer, covered, 20 minutes or until rice is tender and water is absorbed.

2. Add milk, granulated sugar, raisins and apple sauce. Bring to a boil. Reduce heat to low and simmer for 3 minutes, stirring occasionally.

3. Combine cornstarch and remaining ¼ cup water in small bowl. Stir into rice mixture. Simmer about 20 minutes or until mixture thickens, stirring occasionally. Remove from heat; stir in vanilla. Cool 15 to 20 minutes before serving. Sprinkle each serving with brown sugar or nutmeg and garnish with raspberries and orange peel, if desired. Refrigerate leftovers.   *Makes 8 servings*

Nutritional Information per Serving: *Calories: 190, Total Fat: 1 g, Cholesterol: 2 mg, Sodium: 75 mg*

Creamy Rice Pudding

2 cups water
1 cinnamon stick, broken into pieces
1 cup converted rice
4 cups skim milk
¼ teaspoon salt
7¼ teaspoons EQUAL® For Recipes *or*
    24 packets EQUAL® sweetener *or*
    1 cup EQUAL® Spoonful™
3 egg yolks
2 egg whites
1 teaspoon vanilla
¼ cup raisins
    Ground cinnamon and nutmeg

• Heat water and cinnamon stick to boiling in large saucepan; stir in rice. Reduce heat and simmer, covered, until rice is tender and water is absorbed, 20 to 25 minutes. Discard cinnamon stick.

• Stir in milk and salt; heat to boiling. Reduce heat and simmer, covered, until mixture starts to thicken, about 15 to 20 minutes, stirring frequently. (Milk will not be absorbed and pudding will thicken when it cools.) Remove from heat and cool 1 to 2 minutes; stir in Equal®.

• Beat egg yolks, egg whites and vanilla in small bowl until blended. Stir about ½ cup rice mixture into egg mixture; stir back into saucepan. Cook over low heat, stirring constantly, 1 to 2 minutes. Stir in raisins.

• Spoon pudding into serving bowl; sprinkle with cinnamon and nutmeg. Serve warm or at room temperature.
          Makes 6 (⅔-cup) servings

Nutritional Information per Serving: *Calories: 244, Total Fat: 3 g, Cholesterol: 109 mg, Sodium: 200 mg*

Rice Pudding

Tropical Fruit Cream Parfaits

1 cup 2% low-fat milk
1 package (4-serving size) sugar-free
    vanilla instant pudding mix
½ cup mango nectar
    Cinnamon-Ginger Tortilla Sticks
    (recipe follows)
1 large orange, peeled, chopped

1. Pour milk into medium bowl. Add
pudding mix; stir with wire whisk 1 minute
or until smooth and thickened. Stir in
mango nectar; chill.

2. Prepare Cinnamon-Ginger Tortilla Sticks.
Reserve 10 sticks; divide remaining sticks
equally in 5 parfait dishes or small glasses.
Top each with pudding mixture, orange and
two reserved tortilla sticks.

Makes 5 servings

Cinnamon-Ginger Tortilla Sticks

3 tablespoons brown sugar
2 tablespoons margarine
½ teaspoon ground ginger
½ teaspoon ground cinnamon
4 (6-inch) flour tortillas, cut into
    ½-inch strips

1. Preheat oven to 375°F. Combine sugar,
margarine, ginger and cinnamon in small
microwavable bowl. Microwave at HIGH 1
minute or until smooth when stirred.

2. Twist tortillas into spirals and arrange on
baking sheet sprayed with nonstick cooking
spray. Brush each with brown sugar mixture.
Bake 10 to 12 minutes or until edges are
lightly browned; cool.   *Makes 5 servings*

Nutritional Information per Serving: *Calories: 277,
Total Fat: 7 g, Cholesterol: 16 mg, Sodium: 357 mg*

Shamrock Parfaits

1 envelope unflavored gelatin
½ cup cold water
¾ cup sugar
½ cup HERSHEY'S Cocoa
1¼ cups evaporated skim milk
1 teaspoon vanilla extract
2 cups frozen light non-dairy whipped
    topping, thawed, divided
⅛ teaspoon mint extract
6 to 7 drops green food color

In medium saucepan, sprinkle gelatin over
water; let stand 2 minutes to soften. Cook
over low heat, stirring constantly, until
gelatin is completely dissolved, about 3
minutes. In small bowl, stir together sugar
and cocoa; add gradually to gelatin mixture,
stirring with whisk until well blended.
Continue to cook over low heat, stirring
constantly, until sugar is dissolved, about 3
minutes. Remove from heat. Stir in
evaporated milk and vanilla. Pour mixture
into large bowl. Refrigerate, stirring
occasionally, until mixture mounds slightly
when dropped from spoon, about 20
minutes.

Fold ½ cup whipped topping into chocolate
mixture. Divide about half of mixture evenly
among 8 parfait or wine glasses. Stir extract
and food color into remaining 1½ cups
topping; divide evenly among glasses.
Spoon remaining chocolate mixture over
topping in each glass. Garnish as desired.
Serve immediately or cover and refrigerate
until serving time.   *Makes 8 servings*

Nutritional Information per Serving: *Calories: 160,
Total Fat: 3 g, Cholesterol: 0 mg, Sodium: 50 mg*

Tropical Fruit Cream Parfait

Fudgey Chocolate Cupcakes

¾ cup water
½ cup (1 stick) 56-60% corn oil spread, melted
2 egg whites, slightly beaten
1 teaspoon vanilla extract
2¼ cups HERSHEY'S Basic Cocoa Baking Mix (recipe follows)
2 teaspoons powdered sugar
2 teaspoons HERSHEY'S Cocoa (optional)

Heat oven to 350°F. Line 16 muffin cups (2½ inches in diameter) with foil or paper bake cups. In large mixer bowl, stir together water, corn oil spread, egg whites and vanilla. Add Basic Cocoa Baking Mix; beat on low speed of electric mixer until blended. Fill muffin cups ⅔ full with batter.

Bake 20 to 25 minutes or until wooden pick inserted in centers comes out clean. Remove from pans to wire racks. Cool completely. Sift powdered sugar over tops of cupcakes. If desired, partially cover part of each cupcake with paper cutout. Sift cocoa over exposed powdered sugar. Carefully lift off cutout. Store, covered, at room temperature.

Makes 16 cupcakes

Hershey's Basic Cocoa Baking Mix

4½ cups all-purpose flour
2¾ cups sugar
1¾ cups HERSHEY'S Cocoa
1 tablespoon plus ½ teaspoon baking powder
1¾ teaspoons salt
1¼ teaspoons baking soda

In large bowl, stir together all ingredients. Store in airtight container in cool, dry place for up to 1 month. Stir before using.

Makes 8 cups mix

Nutritional Information per Serving (1 cupcake):
Calories: 120, Total Fat: 5 g, Cholesterol: 0 mg, Sodium: 200 mg

Chocolate Peanut Butter Balls

1 cup crunchy peanut butter
1 cup powdered sugar
¼ cup margarine or butter, softened
2 cups KELLOGG'S® RICE KRISPIES® cereal
54 mini-muffin cup papers
1½ cups semi-sweet chocolate morsels
2 tablespoons shortening

In large mixer bowl, combine peanut butter, sugar and margarine on medium speed. Add Kellogg's® Rice Krispies® cereal, mixing until thoroughly combined. Portion mixture, using rounded measuring-teaspoon. Roll into balls. Place each ball in paper cup. Refrigerate.

Melt morsels and shortening in small saucepan, over low heat, stirring constantly. Spoon 1 teaspoon melted chocolate over each peanut butter ball. Refrigerate until firm. Store in airtight container in refrigerator.

Makes 54 peanut butter balls

Nutritional Information per Serving (1 candy):
Calories: 160, Total Fat: 10 g, Cholesterol: 10 mg, Sodium: 80 mg

Fudgey Chocolate Cupcakes

Fudge Brownie Sundaes

1 cup all-purpose flour
¾ cup granulated sugar
½ cup unsweetened cocoa powder, divided
2 teaspoons baking powder
½ teaspoon salt
½ cup skim milk
¼ cup MOTT'S® Natural Apple Sauce
1 teaspoon vanilla extract
1¾ cups hot water
¾ cup packed light brown sugar
½ gallon frozen nonfat vanilla yogurt
Maraschino cherries (optional)

1. Preheat oven to 350°F. Spray 8-inch square baking pan with nonstick cooking spray.

2. In large bowl, combine flour, granulated sugar, ¼ cup cocoa, baking powder and salt. Add milk, apple sauce and vanilla; stir until well blended. Pour batter into prepared pan.

3. In medium bowl, combine hot water, brown sugar and remaining ¼ cup cocoa. Pour over batter. *Do not stir.*

4. Bake 40 minutes or until center is almost set. Cool completely on wire rack. Cut into 12 bars. Top each bar with ½-cup scoop of frozen yogurt; spoon sauce from bottom of pan over yogurt. Garnish with cherry, if desired. *Makes 12 servings*

Nutritional Information per Serving: *Calories: 300, Total Fat: 3 g, Cholesterol: 5 mg, Sodium: 200 mg*

Baked Vanilla Custard

1 quart skim milk
6 eggs
6¼ teaspoons EQUAL® For Recipes *or* 21 packets EQUAL® sweetener *or* ¾ cup plus 2 tablespoons EQUAL® Spoonful™
2 teaspoons vanilla
¼ teaspoon salt
Ground nutmeg

• Heat milk just to boiling in medium saucepan; let cool 5 minutes.

• Beat eggs, Equal®, vanilla and salt in large bowl until smooth; gradually beat in hot milk. Pour mixture into 10 custard cups or 1½-quart glass casserole; sprinkle generously with nutmeg. Place custard cups or casserole in roasting pan; add 1 inch hot water to roasting pan.

• Bake, uncovered, in preheated 325°F oven until sharp knife inserted halfway between center and edge of custard comes out clean, 45 to 60 minutes. Remove custard dishes from roasting pan; cool on wire rack. Refrigerate until chilled.

Makes 10 (½-cup) servings

Nutritional Information per Serving: *Calories: 90, Total Fat: 3 g, Cholesterol: 129 mg, Sodium: 142 mg*

Fudge Brownie Sundae

Caribbean Freeze

⅔ cup sugar
3 tablespoons HERSHEY'S Cocoa
1¾ cups water
3 tablespoons frozen pineapple juice concentrate, thawed
1 tablespoon golden rum *or*
½ teaspoon rum extract

In medium saucepan, stir together sugar and cocoa; stir in water. Cook over medium heat, stirring occasionally, until mixture comes to a boil. Reduce heat; simmer 3 minutes, stirring occasionally. Cool completely. Stir concentrate and rum into chocolate mixture. Cover; refrigerate until cold, about 6 hours. Pour into 1-quart ice cream freezer container. Freeze according to manufacturer's directions. Garnish as desired. *Makes 6 servings*

Nutritional Information per Serving: *Calories: 110, Total Fat: 0 g, Cholesterol: 0 mg, Sodium: 0 mg*

Mocha Sauce

1 cup skim milk
4 teaspoons unsweetened cocoa
2 teaspoons cornstarch
1 teaspoon instant coffee crystals
1 teaspoon vanilla
1¼ teaspoons EQUAL® For Recipes *or*
4 packets EQUAL® sweetener *or*
3 tablespoons EQUAL® Spoonful™

• Combine milk, cocoa, cornstarch and coffee crystals in small saucepan. Cook and stir until thickened and bubbly. Cook and stir 2 minutes more. Remove from heat; stir in vanilla and Equal®. Cool. Cover and chill. *Makes about 1 cup*

Nutritional Information per Serving (1 tablespoon): *Calories: 10, Total Fat: 0 g, Cholesterol: 0 mg, Sodium: 8 mg*

French Vanilla Freeze

10¾ teaspoons EQUAL® For Recipes *or*
36 packets EQUAL® sweetener *or*
1½ cups EQUAL® Spoonful™
2 tablespoons cornstarch
1 piece vanilla bean (2 inches)
⅛ teaspoon salt
2 cups skim milk
2 tablespoons margarine
1 cup real liquid egg product
1 teaspoon vanilla

• Combine Equal®, cornstarch, vanilla bean and salt in medium saucepan; stir in milk and margarine. Heat to boiling over medium-high heat, whisking constantly. Boil until thickened, whisking constantly, about 1 minute.

• Whisk about 1 cup milk mixture into egg product in small bowl; whisk egg mixture back into milk mixture in saucepan. Cook over very low heat, whisking constantly, 30 to 60 seconds. Remove from heat and stir in vanilla. Let cool; remove vanilla bean. Refrigerate until chilled, about 1 hour.

• Freeze mixture in ice cream maker according to manufacturer's directions. Pack into freezer container and freeze until firm, 8 hours or overnight. Before serving, let stand at room temperature until slightly softened, about 15 minutes.

Makes 6 (½-cup) servings

Nutritional Information per Serving: *Calories: 134, Total Fat: 5 g, Cholesterol: 2 mg, Sodium: 205 mg*

Caribbean Freeze

Chocolate-Strawberry Crepes

CREPES

⅔ cup all-purpose flour
2 tablespoons unsweetened cocoa
  powder
6 packages artificial sweetener or
  equivalent of ¼ cup sugar
¼ teaspoon salt
1¼ cups skim milk
½ cup cholesterol-free egg substitute
1 tablespoon margarine, melted
1 teaspoon vanilla
  Nonstick cooking spray

FILLING AND TOPPING

4 ounces fat-free cream cheese,
  softened
1 package (1.3 ounces) chocolate
  fudge-flavored sugar-free instant
  pudding mix
1½ cups skim milk
¼ cup all-fruit strawberry preserves
2 tablespoons water
2 cups fresh hulled and quartered
  strawberries

1. To prepare crepes, combine flour, cocoa, artificial sweetener and salt in food processor; process to blend. Add milk, egg substitute, margarine and vanilla; process until smooth. Let batter stand at room temperature 30 minutes.

2. Spray 7-inch nonstick skillet with cooking spray; heat over medium-high heat. Pour 2 tablespoons crepe batter into hot pan. Immediately rotate pan back and forth to swirl batter over entire surface of pan. Cook 1 to 2 minutes or until crepe is brown around edge and top is dry. Carefully turn crepe with spatula and cook 30 seconds more. Transfer crepe to waxed paper to cool. Repeat with remaining batter, spraying pan with cooking spray as needed. Separate crepes with sheets of waxed paper.

3. To prepare chocolate filling, beat cream cheese in medium bowl with electric mixer at high speed until smooth; set aside. Prepare chocolate pudding with skim milk according to package directions. Gradually add pudding to cream cheese mixture; beat at high speed 3 minutes.

4. To prepare strawberry topping, combine preserves and water in large bowl until smooth. Add strawberries; toss to coat.

5. Spread 2 tablespoons chocolate filling evenly over surface of crepe; roll tightly. Repeat with remaining crepes. Place two crepes on each plate. Spoon ¼ cup strawberry topping over each serving. Serve immediately.

Makes 8 servings (2 crepes each)

Nutritional Information per Serving: *Calories: 161, Total Fat: 2 g, Cholesterol: 1 mg, Sodium: 374 mg*

Raspberry Sauce

2 cups fresh raspberries or thawed
  frozen unsweetened raspberries
1 tablespoon orange juice
1¼ teaspoons EQUAL® For Recipes *or*
  4 packets EQUAL® sweetener *or*
  3 tablespoons EQUAL® Spoonful™
½ teaspoon finely grated orange peel

• Place raspberries in blender container; blend until smooth. Strain through sieve; discard seeds. Stir orange juice, Equal® and orange peel into puréed berries. Serve over fresh fruit, frozen yogurt or cheesecake.

Makes 1 cup

Nutritional Information per Serving (¼ cup): *Calories: 35, Total Fat: 0 g, Cholesterol: 0 mg, Sodium: 0 mg*

Chocolate-Strawberry Crepes

A Lighter Chocolate Decadence

1¼ cups sugar, divided
⅔ cup unsweetened cocoa powder
2 tablespoons all-purpose flour
¾ cup nonfat milk
5 ounces (about ¾ cup) semisweet chocolate chips
¼ cup Prune Purée (page 10) or prepared prune butter
1 egg
1 egg yolk
1 teaspoon vanilla
2 egg whites
⅛ teaspoon cream of tartar
Raspberry Sauce (recipe follows)
1½ cups low-fat nondairy whipped topping
Fresh raspberries and mint leaves for garnish

Preheat oven to 350°F. Line 9-inch round layer cake pan with parchment paper or waxed paper; coat with vegetable cooking spray. In medium saucepan, combine 1 cup sugar, cocoa and flour. Slowly whisk in milk until blended. Bring to a simmer over low heat, stirring constantly. Place chocolate chips in large bowl; pour in hot mixture, stirring until chocolate melts. Whisk in prune purée, egg, egg yolk and vanilla until blended. Set aside to cool. In mixer bowl, beat egg whites with cream of tartar until foamy. Gradually beat in remaining ¼ cup sugar until stiff peaks form. Fold half the egg white mixture into cooled chocolate mixture; fold in remaining egg white mixture. Pour into prepared pan. Bake in center of oven 30 to 35 minutes until puffy and center is set but still moist. *Do not overbake.* Cool completely in pan on wire rack. (Cake will sink as it cools.) Remove from pan. Wrap securely; chill 24 hours before serving. Prepare Raspberry Sauce. Cut dessert into wedges; serve with Raspberry Sauce and whipped topping. Garnish with raspberries and mint leaves. *Makes 12 servings*

Raspberry Sauce: Purée 1 package (12 ounces) thawed frozen raspberries in blender; strain. Sweeten to taste with sugar. Makes 1 cup.

Nutritional Information per Serving: *Calories: 200, Total Fat: 10 g, Cholesterol: 35 mg, Sodium: 30 mg*

Favorite recipe from **California Prune Board**

Pineapple Boats with Citrus Creme

1 large DOLE® Fresh Pineapple
1 DOLE® Banana, peeled, sliced
1 DOLE® Orange, peeled, sliced
1 DOLE® Apple, cored, sliced
1 DOLE® Pear, cored, sliced
1 cup seedless DOLE® Grapes (red and green)

CITRUS CREME

1 cup plain nonfat yogurt
2 tablespoons brown sugar
1 tablespoon minced crystallized ginger, optional
1 teaspoon *each*: grated orange and lime peel

• Cut pineapple in half lengthwise through the crown. Cut fruit from shells, leaving shells intact. Core and chunk fruit.

• Combine pineapple chunks with remaining fruit. Spoon into pineapple boats.

• Combine all ingredients for Citrus Creme. Serve with pineapple boats.

Makes 8 servings

Prep Time: 20 minutes

Nutritional Information per Serving: *Calories: 104, Total Fat: 1 g, Cholesterol: trace, Sodium: 23 mg*

A Lighter Chocolate Decadence

Acknowledgments

The publisher would like to thank the following companies and organizations for the use of their recipes in this publication:

California Prune Board
Dole Food Company, Inc.
Domino Sugar Corporation
Duncan Hines
Egg Beaters® Healthy Real Egg Substitute
Equal® sweetener
Fleischmann's® Original Spread
Hershey Foods Corporation
Kellogg Company
Land O' Lakes, Inc.
MOTT'S® Inc., a division of Cadbury Beverages, Inc.
National Honey Board
New York Apple Association, Inc.
The Quaker® Kitchens
The J.M. Smucker Company